Art Doll Adventures

Exploring Projects and Processes through Cultural Traditions

Lisa Li Hertzi

QUARRY BOOKS

First published in the United States of America by
Quarry Books, a member of
Quayside Publishing Group
33 Commercial Street
Gloucester, Massachusetts 01930-5089
Telephone: (978) 282-9590
Fax: (978) 283-2742
www.quarrybooks.com

Library of Congress Cataloging-in-Publication Data
Hertzi, Lisa Li.
Art doll adventures : exploring projects and processes through cultural traditions / Lisa Li Hertzi.
p. cm.
ISBN-13: 978-1-59253-267-4
ISBN-10: 1-59253-267-5
1. Dollmaking. I. Title.
TT175.H47 2007
745.592'21—dc22 2006038501
CIP

ISBN-13: 978-1-59253-267-4
ISBN-10: 1-59253-267-5

10 9 8 7 6 5 4 3 2 1

Cover Design: Rockport Publishers
Design: Peter M. Blaiwas, Vern Associates
Production: Todd Fairchild
Cover Image: Allan Penn
Photography: Robert Hirsch
Technical Editor: Susan Huxley
Illustrations and Patterns: Lisa Li Hertzi

Printed in Singapore

This book is dedicated to my parents, Judi and Joe Hertzi,
who embrace the creative life with such delighted dedication
that I could not help but follow them on the path of Making and Doing.

Contents

Introduction

Welcome to *Art Doll Adventures*!

I hope you enjoy this adventure through time and around the corners of the globe. We will be traversing the deepest jungles of Africa with Namba Teeke, who sits here as I write, dangling her long legs carelessly off the edge of the table and chattering away. We will canoe the Colorado River hundreds of years ago and walk with the native people in Wupatki. We will explore how to joyfully mangle your patterns, make paper clay faces, make a doll artist trading card (ATC), and nkondi pincushion. In the chapter on the goddess we will shimmy way back in time, thousands of years ago, to find the traditional Bird Goddess, then dance forward, merging her with Our Lady of Guadalupe to create Our Lady of Eureka and, of course, her Blue Chickie of Happiness.

Why all this jumping from time to time, from place to place? Why focus on the past? Because it is just so amazingly rich! And when you bring the past with its iconic splendor in to your present with the delicate gloves of your mind's eye, you may find that this creative journey is in itself, the adventure; perhaps it is not the doll, but the journey to the doll that is the real magic.

Finding meaning in your art is one thing and doing it for the fun of the creation is another. Both are equally juicy and rich. How do they go together? Making dolls with the help of cultural icons brings instant meaning into your work. Your creative flair is of the twenty-first century, but the ideas are primitive and musty with the smell of earth and they are not just yours, they are everyone's. They are in our blood, and they connect us. As you are exploring this book, look into other books on the subjects that excite you. For inspiration, surf the 'net, go to galleries, and browse your favorite shops seeking out new colors, shapes, and texture.

And one very important thing—do not take this process too seriously! Do let it get under your skin and make you think and learn; don't let the details get in the way. We have included instructions to make each of these dolls stitch by stitch, but there are also creativity exercises to nudge you along a different path, to point you toward different tools, wild materials, and unique methods. I encourage you to prowl through this book, look at all of the wonderful gallery samples, skip pages, stop and read, fold your favorite pages over, crack it open so the spine lets go of its strangle hold on the pages and lays flat, and then pick a project. All of these dolls can be done in snippets of time here and there, in one passionate fell swoop or . . . as you please.

Be fearless! Play with abandon!

Should you get lost and forget either of those things, here are some ideas to get you and your doll back onto the playground.

- Get or make a sketchbook that you love and start recording your thoughts and inspirations. Fill it with fabric swatches, doodles, and mangled patterns, and use it to record the adventure. (More on this later!)
- Write a story for your doll.
- Do it! Get in the way of inspiration by sitting down and getting started.
- Cut out two patterns of a doll in different fabrics and make them up at the same time, and see how different they are!
- Learn new and interesting things.
- Go shopping for delicious fabric and art supplies.
- Take a walk as your doll.
- Borrow skills from yourself, say . . . knitting or carving horns and use them in your doll.
- Look with a fresh eye and no mind and you will see what is there, not what you think is there . . . and it will surprise you.
- Make accessories for your doll, or make it an environment.
- Play with your doll, really play!
- Be mischievous and curious, ask questions and be totally open to the answers you get.
- Go see art, a movie, the ocean, your neighborhood.
- Remember, skills evolve. Be easy on yourself and keep the catastrophes . . . they remind you how far you have come.
- And finally, have fun!

Gather the basic equipment and supplies.

This chapter will discuss your core supplies: fabrics, sewing machines, needles, threads, and the beading and embellishment materials that you will need to complete the projects. The materials are divided in to "kits" that you can assemble and have ready when you are ready to create. It is wonderful to have an inspiration and be able to reach over and easily pick up the tools you need to express it! The kits are named with the obvious in mind; Embellishing Kit, Painting and Drawing Kit, Sculpting Kit, and most important, the Basics Kit. In each chapter there are also Adventurers materials lists that will have additional goodies for you to discover! This list suggests ingredients that will take your beautiful dolls and make them magnificent. You are encouraged to embellish and experiment as you work through the bonus project in each chapter.

Most important, just remember that dolls are fun! Art is fun! Life is fun! Have fun as you explore this book.

Chapter 1:

Getting Started

Supplies, Patterns, Embroidery Basics, and Keeping a Journal

Fabrics

"Fiberholic" and "Firmly Stuffed" have all made it to the bumper of my car at some point in time. If you are a fiber fanatic, you need no prodding, just go find it, go get it, go make it! The perfect fabric is such a juicy start to your doll, so pick the fabric that calls to you. Play!

Here are some handy hints. Remember that stuffing migrates and a very porous fabric will bleed white fuzz. Choose 100% cotton with a tight weave for most of the basic bodies of all of these dolls. Remember that knits will stretch, which might be just what you were looking for, but maybe not. Note the two examples at right. Both were made from the exact same pattern, but Gracie Ann (left) is constructed from a tight-weave velvet and Benjamin (right) is from four-way stretch, heavy-duty cycling-shorts Lycra.

A head can be made from stretch fabric . . . or not.

Remember sheer fabrics are delicious for decoration and dresses, but might tear if used as a body fabric. Thick fabrics are a bear to turn right side out, but as Cody Goodin exhibits in the Gallery (page 40), they can be well worth the effort.

Tip

Some of these dolls can be made without any fabric at all (and you will see examples where this is the case). Remember to think circles around your past. In other words, know that there is value in your experiences but do not allow these to anchor you to your past. Listen to the pattern, but follow your instinct of the moment!

Sewing Machine

Many doll makers have a passionate love affair with their sewing machine, so I would never presume to give you advice on what to use when you are making dolls. Some people swear by the fancy digital machines that embroider, speak to you in French, and calculate pi while submitting your tax forms. Others are in love with their 1920s Singers that move along with a comforting clunkety clunk. For the doll projects in this book, all you need is a reliable straight stitch that travels both forward and backward, but never underestimate the joys of new toys and the new Maserati-esque machines with their variable speeds, computerized art functions, and other goodies that may spur you in to another creative universe.

A mix of hand and machine sewing works best for these projects. A fun approach is to create the basic doll with some quick machine sewing, which also prevents stuffing from poking out, and then add some stitch personality by hand sewing and decorative stitching over and around the secure machine seams.

If you choose to create your doll solely with hand stitching, here are a few suggestions.

When the instructions tell you to sew, you can use a ladder stitch (page 16). Or, so you do not end up with stuffing poking through the seams, try using a blanket stitch (page 15) with the fabric right side out, being careful to make the stitches tight and neat as they will be in plain view. You can also start with right sides together, using a running stitch as you would if you were using the machine (as shown below), then turn them right side out and do a decorative stitch on the outside to nip that fiber migration in the bud. Make the decorative stitch interesting by using a contrasting thread or tug the stitches as you work, to make a nice scrumply ridge.

Tip

For dolls, Mountain Mist is superior to any other polyester stuffing. It is not slippery and it stays together. This stuffing does not leave shreds all over the place before the job is done. It packs nice and tight and the fiber is not prone to migration. But it can get lumpy if you are not careful. If you are terrified of doll "cellulite," use Fairfield Poly-fil.

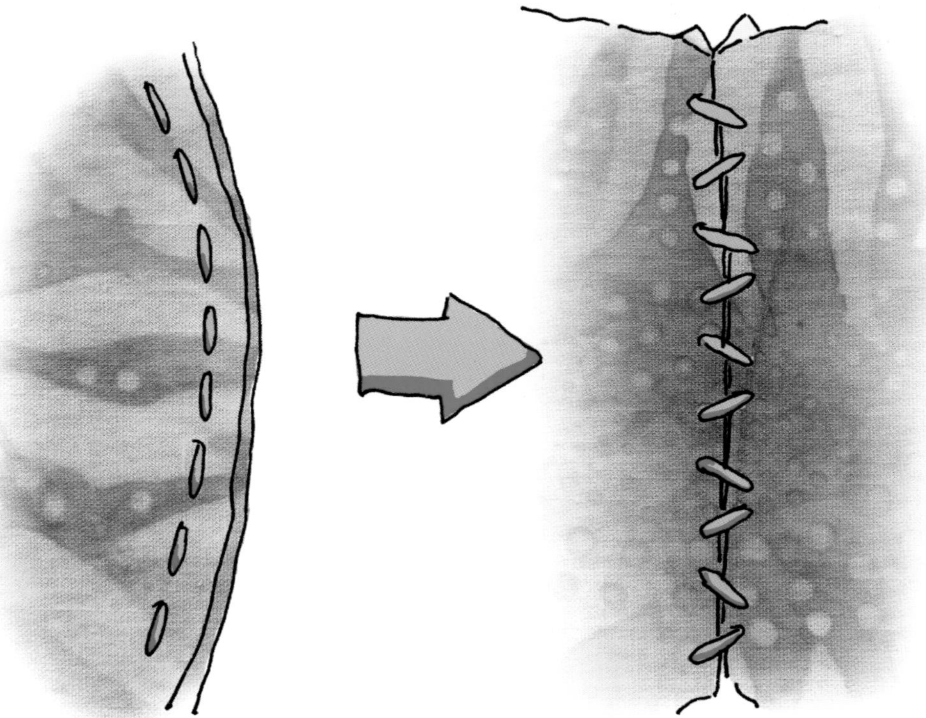

Running stitch with right sides together

Decorative stitching on the outside of a seam

General Supplies

In addition to glorious fabric and your favorite sewing machine, you will need to gather a few more basic supplies. There are two supply lists at the front of each chapter; one list called Materials and another called Tools. These give you all the ingredients that you need to put the doll together, and your creation will be beautiful!

To get you started, in this chapter you will find lists of basic supplies and equipment. Called kits, they include items that you should have on hand when you start any of the projects in this book.

Basics Kit

- polyester stuffing such as Mountain Mist Fiberloft or Fairfield Premium Polyester Fiberfill
- polyester thread (Note: Use 100% polyester for seaming any fabric pieces that will be stuffed so that the stitching, which will be under stress, will not break.)
- decorative threads: cotton, embroidery, and metallic
- doll-sculpting needles: 3 ½" (8.9 cm) for everyday use and a 5" (12.7 cm) for extra reach
- hand-sewing needle
- sewing machine
- sewing machine accessories: bobbins, needles
- various presser feet for decorative stitching (optional)
- cardboard and paper or quilter's template material for pattern piece templates
- tracing paper
- iron and ironing surface
- liquid seam sealer such as Dritz Fray Check
- permanent spray adhesive for mounting patterns
- pinking sheers
- Sanford Prismacolor (Karisma internationally) colored pencils for tracing patterns and marking fabric
- scissors
- seam ripper
- straight pins
- tape measure
- thimble
- thread lubricant such as Sewer's Aid
- bow whip for turning large areas
- finger-turning tools such as Keeling's Krafts/Dolls To Do Tiny Turning Tubes and Turn-It-All Tube Turner
- hemostats for turning fabric pieces
- stuffing fork or wood dowel with a point

Sculpting Kit

- paper clay such as Creative Paperclay or Delight Modeling Compound
- cotton cloth
- craft knife such as X-Acto
- mat knife
- modeling tools: sharp point and blunt edge
- plastic surface to work on
- ruler
- white craft glue that dries clear, such as Elmer's Glue
- container of water

Embellishing Kit

- collage materials: found objects, photos, pictures, printed ephemera, tissue paper, and words
- tulle slightly larger than desired collage dimensions
- unique and wonderful scraps of fabric, paper, and yarn
- interesting buttons and fibers
- beaded fringe, lace, ribbon, upholstery fringe, and snippets of other interesting trims
- beads of all kinds
- beading needle that fits through the holes in your preferred beads
- beading thread such as Nymo (Note: You can use other types of thread, but they will not be as reliable or as easy to work with.)
- craft wire in various colors
- glue gun and glue sticks
- paper towels
- white craft glue that dries clear, such as Elmer's Glue

Painting and Drawing Kit

- acrylic craft paint: medium- to high-viscosity such as any type from Liquitex, DecoArt SoSoft Fabric Acrylics, and Jacquard Dye-Na-Flow and Lumiere
- gesso
- Liquitex Matte Gel Medium or Plaid Mod Podge
- cotton cloth for smudging paint
- polyurethane for sealing fabric and wood
- textile paints
- colored pencils, pens, and crayons
- fine-lead pencil for marking paint locations
- paintbrushes with a variety of tips for applying gesso and details
- paper towels
- sandpaper
- Sharpie pens in a variety of weights and colors
- working mount (page 19)
- calligraphy or dip pen such as Speedball Crow Quill and ink
- watercolor pencils
- sketchbook
- container for mixing gesso with water, sand, or other items
- container of water for rinsing paintbrushes, thinning and mixing paint, and rubbing paint off a surface

Using the Patterns

If you like to use your pattern pieces over and over, then start by creating cardboard templates. First photocopy or trace the pattern pieces on to lightweight paper. Coat the back of the paper with a permanent spray adhesive and press the paper, tracing side up, on to noncorrugated cardboard. Now cut the pieces from the paper and cardboard sandwich. This will make tracing easy and more accurate.

If desired, you can trace shapes directly on to quilter's template material, which is somewhat transparent.

Most of the patterns on pages 114–124 are provided without seam allowances. Where they are excluded, you do not need them because you are going to trace the pattern pieces onto your fabric, sew on the fabric along the lines, and then cut out the shapes. You will create the seam allowances by your cutting action. With one exception (Our Lady of Eureka), it is best to use 1/8" (3 mm) -wide seam allowances.

Some of the pattern pieces have seam allowances built in, and are marked to indicate this, so be sure to read the labels on the pattern pieces carefully.

Tip

My collection of paintbrushes includes a 1" (2.5 cm) flat and a variety of smaller tips. I use Winsor & Newton University Series 233. They have great tips and survive the abuse of painting fabric, poking into holes, and other strange things. You might want to get a #4, #8, and #0, #00, or #000, depending on the intensity of your love affair with detail.

After tracing pattern piece shapes onto your fabric with a contrasting color pencil (Sanford Prismacolor pencils work the best), you can cut out pattern pieces with pinking shears.

There are many curves in these patterns. When instructions tell you to cut little Vs, you need to snip through the seam allowance, close to the stitching, around the curves, and in the bends. Here is an illustration of good snipping around our Wupatki doll (a).

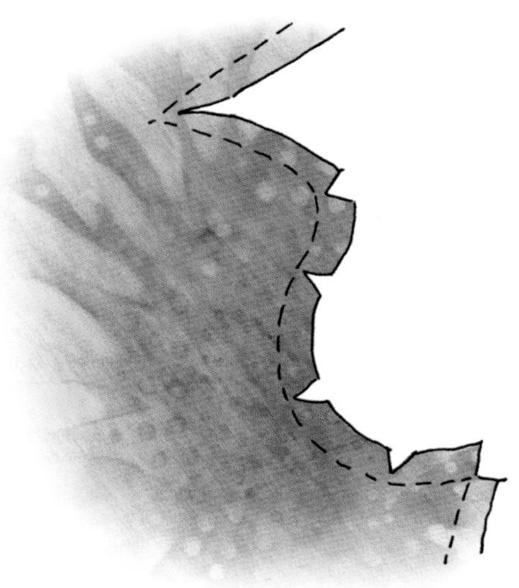

(a)
Vs cut in to the seam allowances help a curved seam conform to the desired shape.

Embellishing with Embroidery

As you work on your creation, here are some handy stitches you will use time and again. Step-by-step instructions guide you through the stitches that are used in the projects in this book.

Backstitch

If you want to outline something, this is the perfect stitch. Try this one on Kondi's teeth (chapter 3) and the eyes for the Most High Sun Bird Goddess (chapter 5).

1. Bring the thread up from behind at A, insert needle at B, and come out at C (b).
2. Reenter at A and come out at D to repeat the process (c).

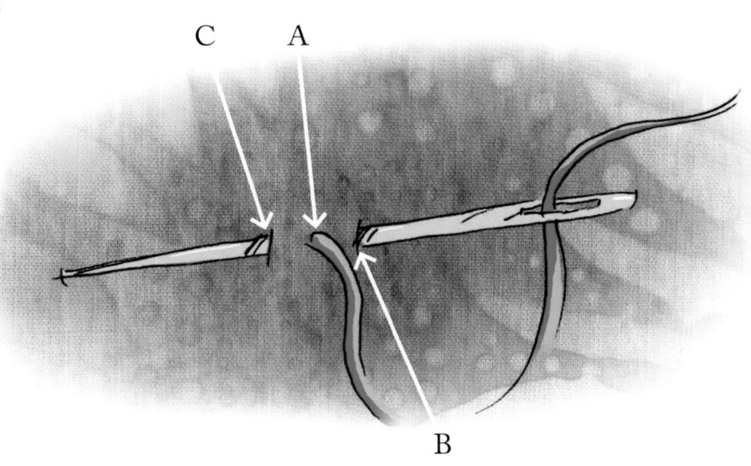

(b)
Start the backstitch with a small stitch in the opposite direction you want to travel.

Tip

To hide thread in a doll, finish off your stitch with a knot. With the needle still threaded, stick the needle into the doll and come out as far from the knot as you can. Pull the thread taut and snip right where it exits the body. The thread will be in the body and totally hidden forever!

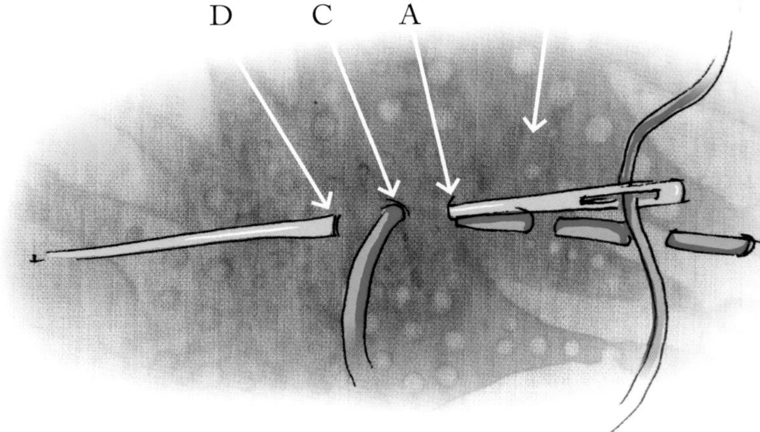

(c)
Make the distance from B to C twice that of A to B.

Blanket Stitch

This is a favorite for edging! You might want to use this for the screen on page 55, or for an eyeball or decorative leaf on a doll.

1. Make an invisible stitch on the wrong side of the work to secure the end of the thread. Working from left to right, bring the needle and thread over the fabric edge, from the back of the work to the front at A. Go in at B and come out at C.
2. Pull taut, being careful to keep the lower thread behind the needle (d).

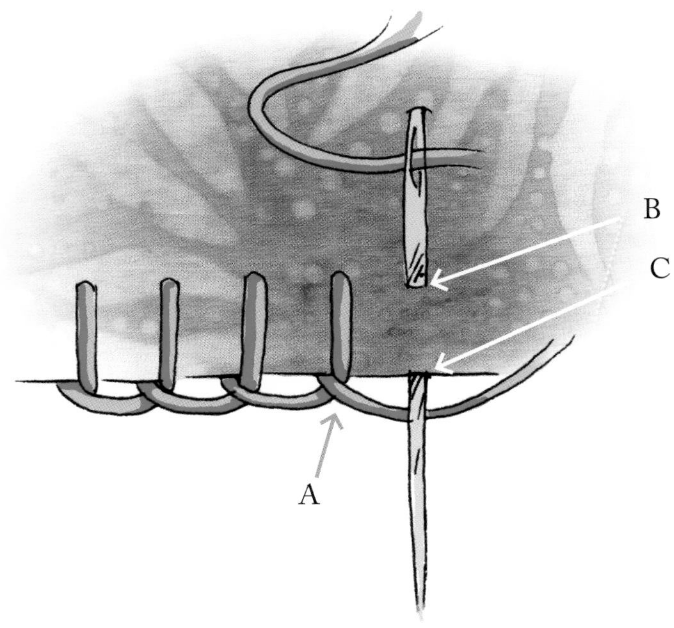

(d)
For each subsequent blanket stitch, move slightly to the right and insert the needle beside B.

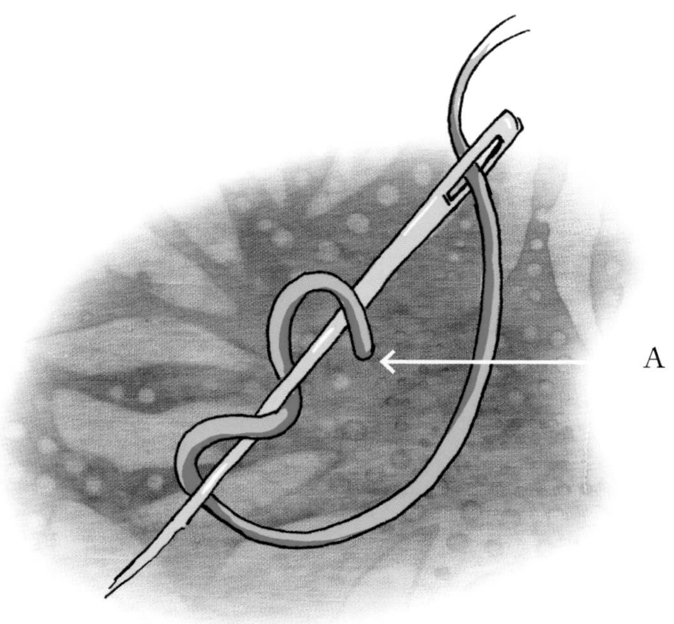

(e)
Insert the needle a few threads to one side of A if the French knot threatens to pop through the hole.

French Knot

The French knot can be dangerously addictive. It creates a mossy texture when stitched densely and is great anywhere a dot is needed.

1. Bring the needle through the fabric at A. Wrap the thread around the needle twice while holding the thread taut with your left hand.
2. Insert the needle back in to A (e).

Ladder Stitch

Use this for closing seams or sculpting. The finished stitches can be hidden or exposed.

1. With both sides of the fabric folded under and carefully pushed together, come up through A, and insert into B (f).

2. Run the needle forward and come out at C, insert into D, run the needle forward to E and over to F (f). Continue this way until you are finished.

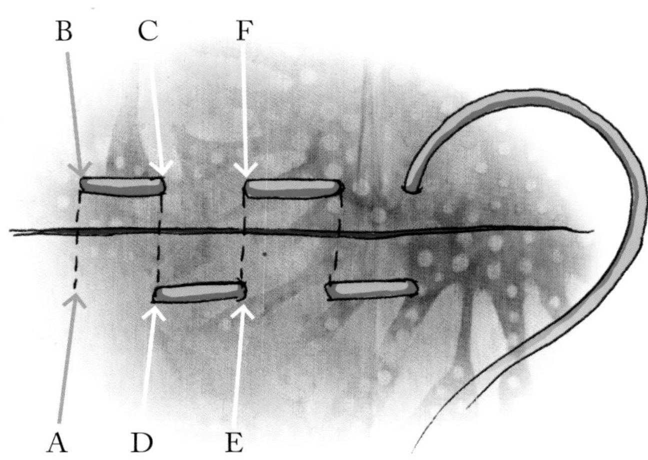

(f)
To hide ladder stitches, position them inside the folded edges.

Long and Short Stitch

This stitch is great for filling in big spaces, as well as making blends.

1. Starting at the far left, make a small stitch. Right next to it, make a stitch that is twice as long as the first (g). Continue along in this manner, until you reach the end.

2. Work the next row in the opposite direction. This time, use only the longer stitches (h). The stitches will end up naturally alternating between long and short.

3. Continue working rows back and forth until you have filled in the shape. After the last row, there are little spaces where the short stitches do not reach the bottom. Use short stitches to fill those spots.

4. Finish with two backstitches and then hide the embroidery thread inside the doll.

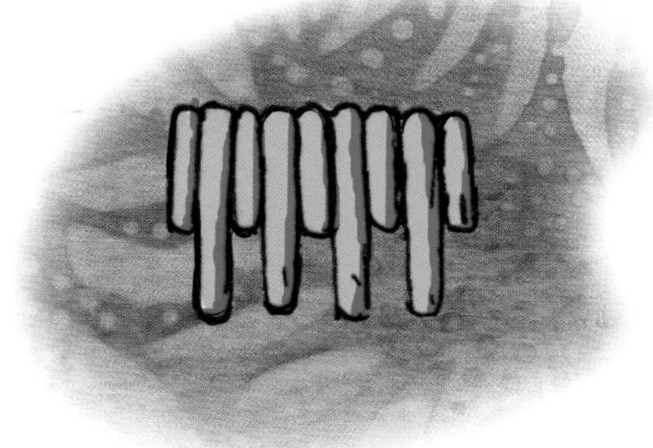

(g)
Alternate two lengths for the long and short stitch.

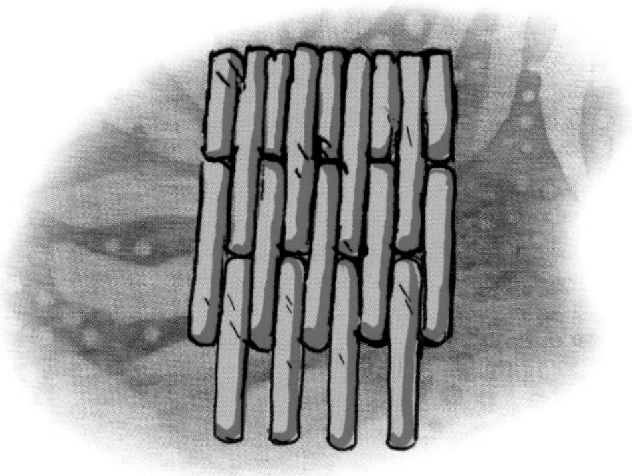

(h)
After the first row, use one stitch length.

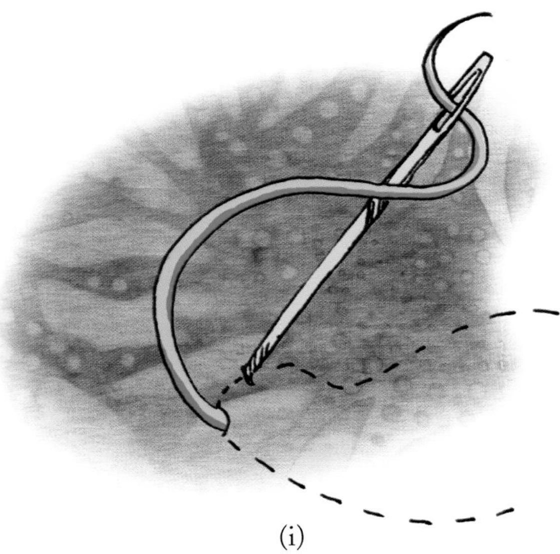

(i)
Make satin stitches from left to right in your shape.

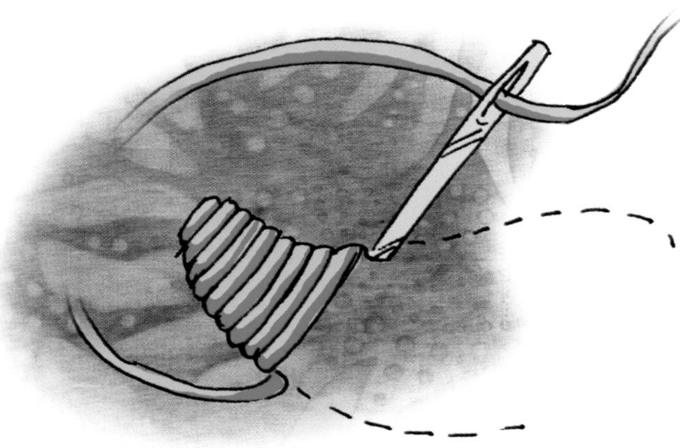

(j)
Stitches can be any length, but they must be side by side.

Satin Stitch

The satin stitch is the universal filler. It is so elegantly simple.

1. Draw the shape you want to fill and bring your needle up at the bottom left (i).
2. Insert the needle at the top of the shape, directly above the place where you came out.
3. Continue making stitches in the same way, laying them very close together, but not overlapping. Hide the background fabric completely (j).

Split Running Stitch

This is a lovely, vintage stitch. It curves beautifully and, when worked densely, can be blended with ease.

1. Starting behind the work, come out at A. Insert the needle at B. Come out at C (k).
2. Bring the needle to the right and insert it in to the center of the first stitch, at D, and come out to the far left, past C (l). Repeat this process to the end.

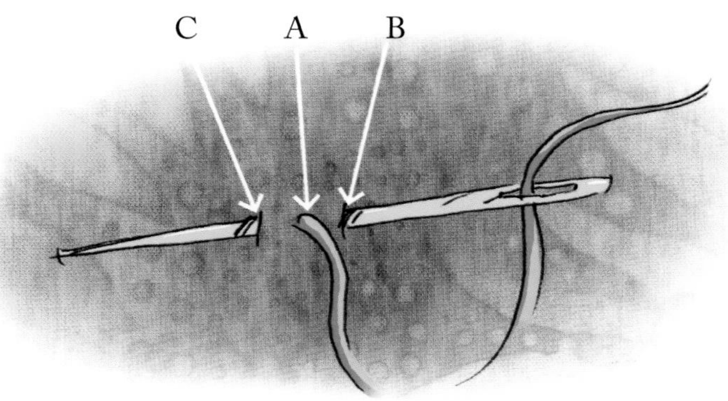

(k)
As the split stitch name implies, each new stitch is made through the previous one.

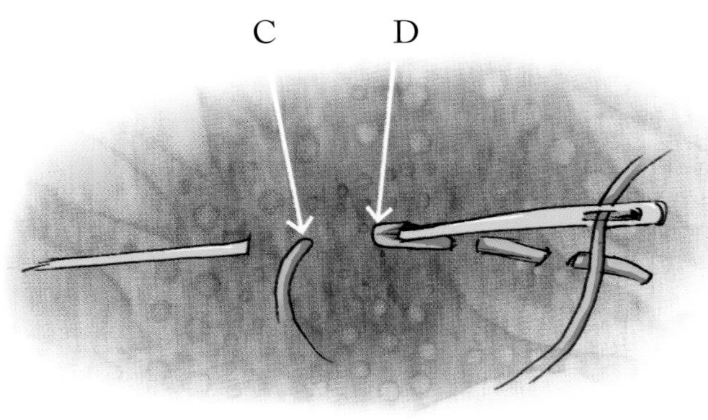

(l)
Continue using the same stitch length.

Creativity Exercise:

Developing a Doll Journal

I always encourage my students to keep a journal, which I like to call a "doll book." It is the tome that will house all of your musings, ideas, inspirations, and your swatch-infested yearnings. But most of all, your doll book is the witness to the evolution of your ideas.

You can create an exquisite doll journal of your own like Kathy Kenny (page 81) and Linda Hansen (page 110–111). Kathy's cover is fabric and it explodes with renegade yarns, is tattooed with interesting grommets, and is sewn, glued, drawn in, written in, and stamped! It is wild and beautiful.

Linda's is equally rich, with its deckle-edged pages, each a different color, and full of photos and musings. The face sketches and collage are wonderful—but Linda's magic is in her writing, so personal that I stopped reading like you would if you discovered your sister's diary, until after a moment of pause, when, of COURSE you would read the rest!

There are many wonderful books out there on making your own blank books. Several of my favorites are listed in the back of this book. I encourage you to try to make one of your own, but if you are tempted by a delicious store-bought journal or sketchbook, buy a nice one.

I usually decorate the covers and name my doll books. As I go through the process of developing and making a doll, I start collecting. I sketch into the book, write, paste, sew, and paint. Very often I make the outline in fabric and play with colors. Always, I put in a pocket where I can hide the art and inspiration that I do not want the world to see just yet. It is great fun to keep this kind of journal, and you may find a whole other creation emerging from between its covers!

Stem Stitch

This is a great outlining stitch. You can create a slender or thicker line by changing the angle of the stitch.

1. Bring the needle through the fabric at A.
2. Insert the needle in at B and come out at C, which is one-third to half of the way back toward A (m). Pull the threads snug so that the longer A-B stitch is below B-C.
3. Holding the thread down as before, repeat to the end (n).

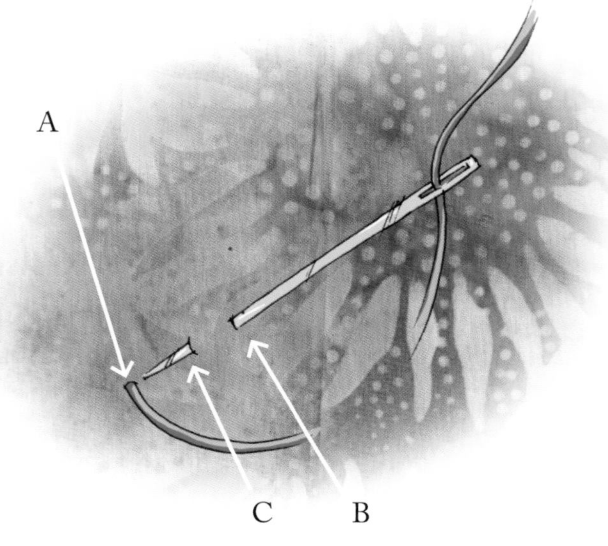

(m)
Make a long and then a short stitch for the stem stitch.

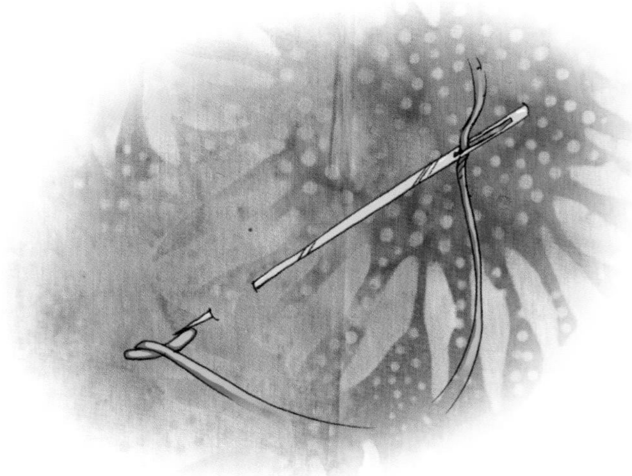

(n)
Overlap each stitch.

Straight Stitch

This is the best of all possible stitches, the height of simplicity! Use it for everything.

1. Come from the back to the front, make a stitch, and repeat.
2. Stitch in a straight line, with uniform or irregular stitch lengths (o).

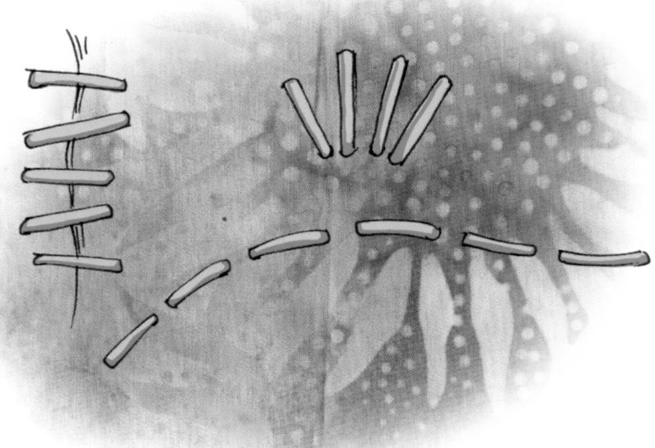

(o)
Make your straight stitches any length and work in any direction.

Creativity Exercise: **Working Mount**

Have you ever fumbled with a small object that you are trying to paint? A mount will save you so much grief because it is good for everything that needs drying. The mount is easy to make, as explained here. This one fits nicely in a small work space, plus the soft pine is lightweight and easy to drill.

Simply use a drill with a ¼" (6 mm) bit to make a hole in the top center of a 7" (17.8 cm) square, soft pine fence topper. Toppers are sold at hardware stores.

Mount whatever you want to paint on a length of ¼" (6 mm) dowel, and pop the opposite end of the dowel in to the hole in the fence topper.

I have always had colorful dreams of Africa. An armchair Africa. A place of deep ceremony, story, inspiration, and most of all, vivid, gritty, dark, vibrant colors: the obvious red, yellow, green, black, the not-so clichéd blue sky, golden-brown sand, hanging-basket dirt, and monochromatic earth colors. This colorful place is in my head only, safe from the ravages of politics, never touched by hunger, and, of course, without the stifling heat! This doll came from *that* Africa.

Chapter 2: Dreaming

2006
numba
·TEEKE·

Namba Teeke: Awakening an African Spirit

African mask from Pablo Picasso's collection.

THIS DOLL EVOLVED, AS MOST OF MY DOLLS DO, through a winding path of looking and listening, reading and sketching, and waiting. Waiting, because these creations come to me gradually, inching along like the consistent, boring earthworm of history, taking what feels like forever, then astounding me with the sudden tornado of ideas, shapes, color, and being! Art is not for the faint of heart.

While I was waiting, I found a wonderfully simple mask in a book about African art. It nestled into my memory until I was looking through a catalogue of Picasso's African art collection and there it was again. "Nice head," I thought, "but what about the body?"

I went back to the same book in which I'd found the mask and found a photo of a helmet mask from Liberia. I noticed to my delight that there were some pretty big feet poking out from the reed skirts that guaranteed that the focus would be on the mask rather than the body of the dancer. Wow!

Not being one to ignore the nagging of inspiration I began sketching . . . and the tornado arrived!

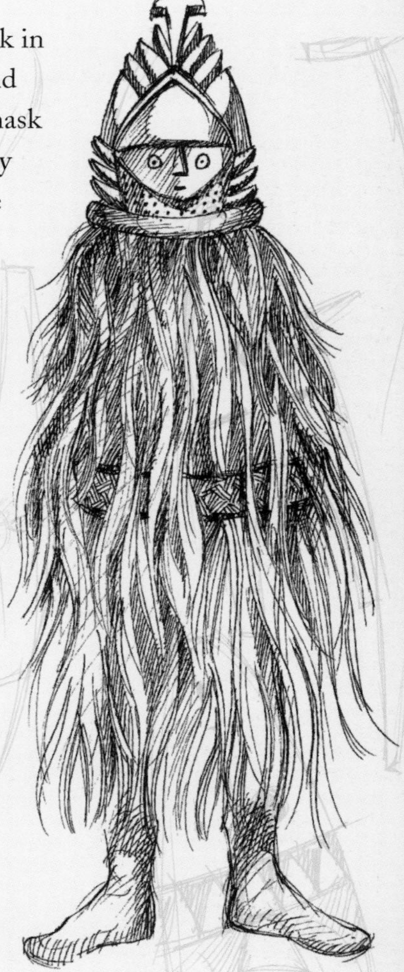

Make your starting point a review of all the instructions for this doll. You want to first understand the process, and then let your own ideas emerge so that you can make this doll uniquely yours. As you are making this doll, I encourage you to look at African art and find African fabric: absorb the colors, study the masks, read the myths, hunt and gather, wait and watch. Do not forget the magic of merging—let a version of your doll emerge that includes your story, your truth, your colors. Let it evolve!

Creativity Exercise:

Joyful Pattern Mangling 101

The point of this creative exercise is to get you thinking of your pattern pieces (pages 114–115) as more than a rigid set of shapes that you must use exactly as presented.

Make a few extra copies and study your patterns. We all have an idea about what a pattern is for and what it should look like. But a pattern is only the structure for what will emerge. Here is a delightfully freeing exercise: joyfully mangle your pattern! By looking at it as a graphic element rather than a "pattern" you may find inspiration coming from a wholly different place than you are accustomed to. Below are a few suggestions, along with some samples of what I did to mine.

- Paint them with watercolor paints
- Paint them with acrylics
- Paint them with fabric dye, wad them up so that the paint creates darker lines in the wrinkles, let dry, and then unwad them and iron
- Glue them to something
- Use wallpaper paste to decorate them
- Sew all over them
- Collage them
- Use them for artist trading cards after you cut them into 2"× 3" (5 × 7.6 cm) squares
- Send them to your friends and have a pattern-reuniting party
- Use stamps and puff paint to decorate them
- Scan them into your computer and use Adobe PhotoShop to add color and shapes to them
- Print them out on a piece of fabric
- Cut them into strips and weave them into a little pattern blanket

Finally, when satisfied that you have surprised yourself completely in this new treatment of a sewing pattern, cut a new pattern out so you can use them to make this doll.

Musings

You may use the colors you discovered while joyfully mangling your pattern or you may use another method to choose your fabric, but remember, the colors and texture of the fabric will be the key to whether she tangos or pirouettes, stalks into the night or smiles.

Materials

- basics, embellishing, painting and drawing, and sculpting kits (page 12)
- two fat quarters of fabric for the body, legs, arms, head, foot pad, and snoot (Note: Use a light cotton backing if there is a chance stuffing will seep through.)
- 2" (5.1 cm) contrasting fabric for the undernose
- 2" (5.1 cm) square of plain fabric for both eyes
- matching sewing thread
- three strips of tulle or other sheer or lightweight fabric, each 2" × 15" (5.1 × 38.1 cm) for the puff
- one ball of very fluffy yarn for the puff
- one ball of eyelash or similar yarn of contrasting color and texture for the puff
- two beads for eye pupils, both smaller than the eyeball
- 1/4" to 1/2" (6 mm to 1.3 cm) -long, 1/8" (3 mm) thick red bead for mouth or embroidery thread: red, a dark for outlining, and white for teeth
- 4" (10.2 cm) -long, 1/4" (6 mm) wood dowel for the rigid neck (optional)
- matching paint for dowel of the rigid neck (optional)

Tools

- air- or water-erasable pen or pencil for the mouth

Adventurer's Materials

- basic head without a snoot, lightly stuffed and temporarily mounted on a dowel
- beads, collage, and yarn for embellishing
- Liquitex Natural Sand Texture Gel
- paint for face
- puff paints

Preparing the Pattern

1. Trace the pattern pieces (pages 114–115) onto cardboard and cut them out.
2. Lay the two pieces of body fabric right sides together. Trace two each of the leg, body, and arm pattern pieces on to the upper fabric. Trace the head, foot pad, and snoot once. On a single piece of contrasting fabric, trace the undernose. Trace and cut the eyes from plain fabric.
3. Cut out the bodies, foot pads, eyes, undernose, and a piece 1¼" × 3½" (3.2 × 8.9 cm) for the headband. Put these aside.
4. Following the traced lines, sew together the pattern pieces to make the arms, head, and legs. Leave open where indicated. Sew around the entire head, without leaving an opening. With the right sides together, sew together the longest, straight edge of the snoot, to make the bridge.
5. Cut around the arms, head, and legs. Be careful to snip in to the space where the ears meet the head and the pointy area on the paw.

Tip

Backstitch at the beginning and end of the seams where the openings are noted on the arm and leg. You will be stuffing through there and may notice the stitching unraveling a bit if you have not attended to this little detail.

Arms

1. Turn the arms right side out. Turn under the top ¼" (6 mm) and pin, but do not sew. Stuff from the middle toward the top very firmly. Stuff the paws less firmly.
2. Make a hidden knot by coming in through the side at the triangle and making a knot. Following the dashed line, hand stitch back and forth through the paw, pulling tightly as you go (a). Make a small knot in the thread, at the wrist.

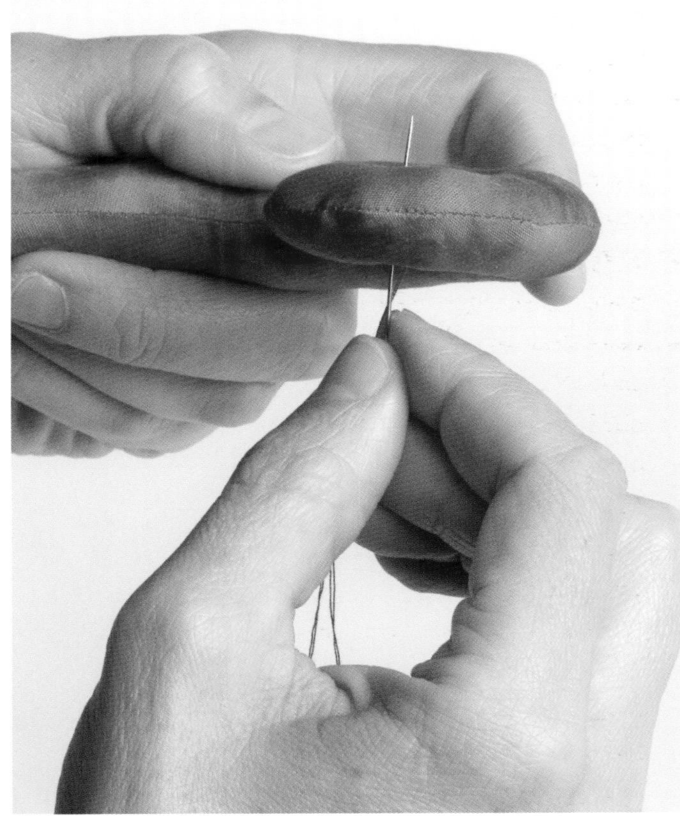

(a)
For sculpting, insert the needle through the flat side of the hand.

Legs

1. With right sides together, pin a foot pad to the bottom of a leg, matching the triangles (b).

2. Sew all of the way around the foot.

3. Turn the legs right side out. Turn the top of each leg under ½" (1.3 cm) and pin, but do not sew. Stuff the leg firmly.

Musings

Do you want the feet to be heavy dancing feet? If so, fill a little plastic bag with sand, shot, or rocks, then stuff the bottom of the foot with a ¼" (6 mm) layer of stuffing, insert the little bag, then stuff around it and finish stuffing the full length of the leg.

(b)
Pin and sew a foot pad to the bottom of each leg.

Head

1. Cut a 1¼" (3.2 cm) vertical opening in the back of the head. Turn the head right side out and stuff it firmly. Do not sew head closed.

2. Cut out the snoot. With the right sides together, match the triangles on the snoot and undernose and sew along two sides of the undernose (c). Turn the joined pieces right side out

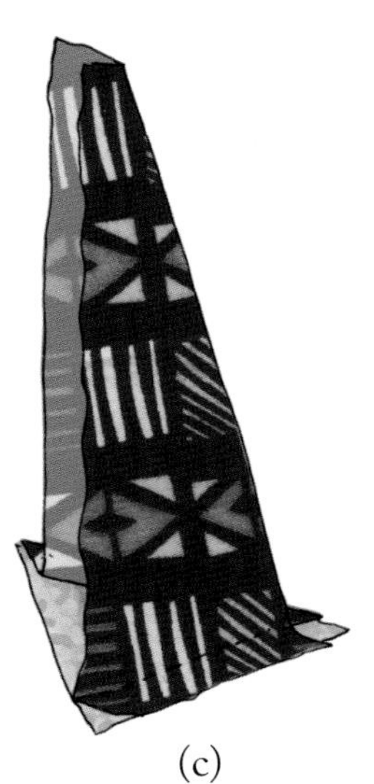

(c)
Sew the undernose.

3. Fold the long sides of the headband fabric under ¼" (6 mm). Sew onto the head just under where the ears meet the forehead, like a headband.

4. Roll some stuffing on to your stuffing tool and lay it along the inside of the open snoot, and pull the tool out while leaving the stuffing behind, thus creating a tight roll of stuffing. Stuff around the roll.

5. Loosely turn the unseamed edges under and stitch the back of the nose closed (d).

6. Pin the snoot to the head. Sew it on to the head, leaving the top open.

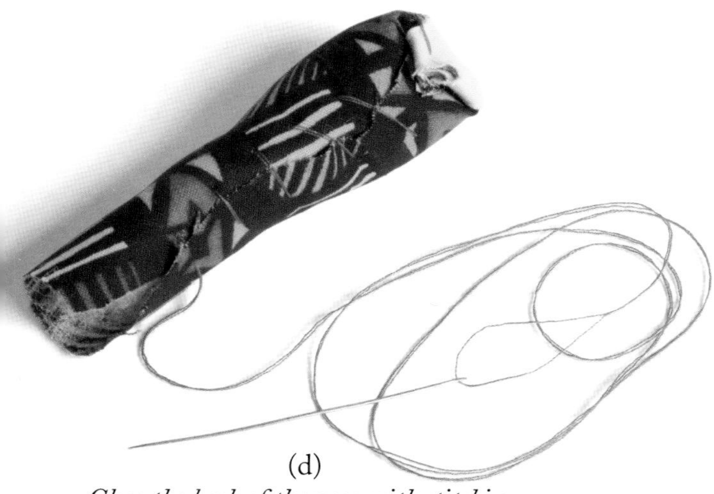

(d)
Close the back of the nose with stitching.

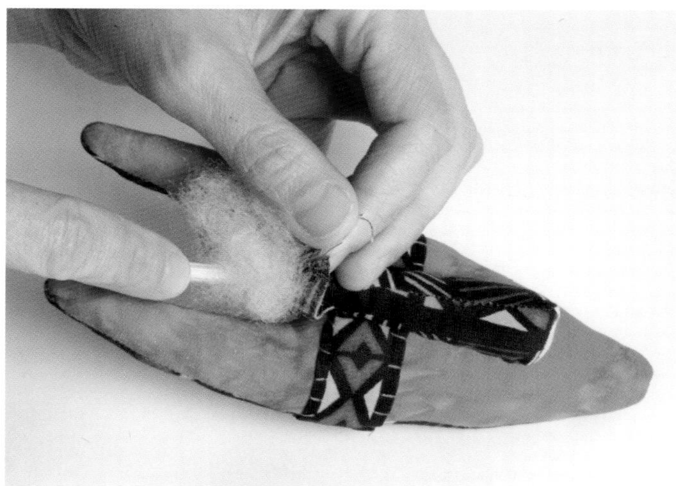

(e)
Sew snoot to head.

7. Add more stuffing inside the snoot, through the top, until it is firmly stuffed (e). Turn the extra fabric under and sew the top of the snoot closed.

8. Use a blanket (page 15) or straight (page 19) stitch to sew the eyes to the head. Sew beads in the center of the eyes, for pupils.

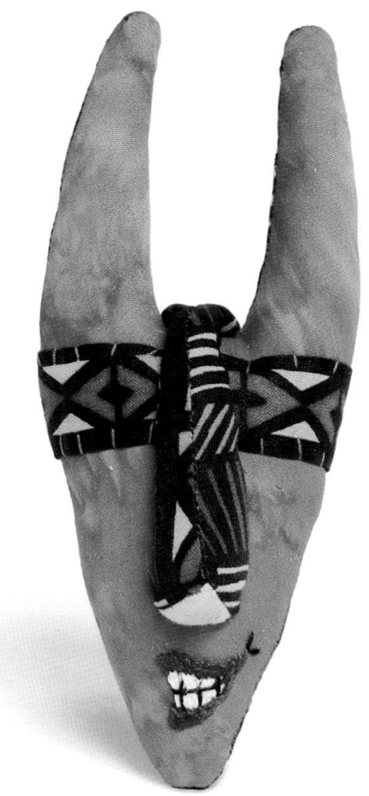

Tip

Play with the personality by changing the snoot: is it a real beak? Or, with just a slight change in elevation, does it conjure an image of Jimmy Durante or of Piglet? If you want the point of the nose to be prominent, choose a small bead, thread it, and tie a knot. Now bring the needle from the inside of the snoot to the outside at the tip, turn the needle around, make a tiny stitch, go back into the snoot, and restring the bead that's inside. Tie off the thread. Now stuff the snoot. You will not have that annoying unstuffed space at the tip, which sometimes happens with just stuffing.

Another handy trick for getting your nose to have that perky tip is to use white glue. Put a dab on your pointy stuffing tool. Insert the tool into the snoot and squeeze the snoot from the outside, distributing the glue inside the snoot. Immediately roll a little ball of stuffing onto the end of your stuffing tool and push it into the glued area. Squeeze snoot again from the outside and stuff as usual.

9. To create a simple bead mouth, find a long red bead and sew it on to the doll. To create an embroidered mouth, trace a mouth shape (f) onto your doll head with an air- or water-erasable pen or pencil. (Test the pen or pencil on a fabric scrap to make sure that the marks do disappear. Take care, because the marks made by some products will reappear over time.) Choose a red, a white, and a dark outlining color for the embroidery thread. Use all six of the plies in a strand when embroidering. Use a satin stitch for the teeth and a stem stitch for the outlines (f).

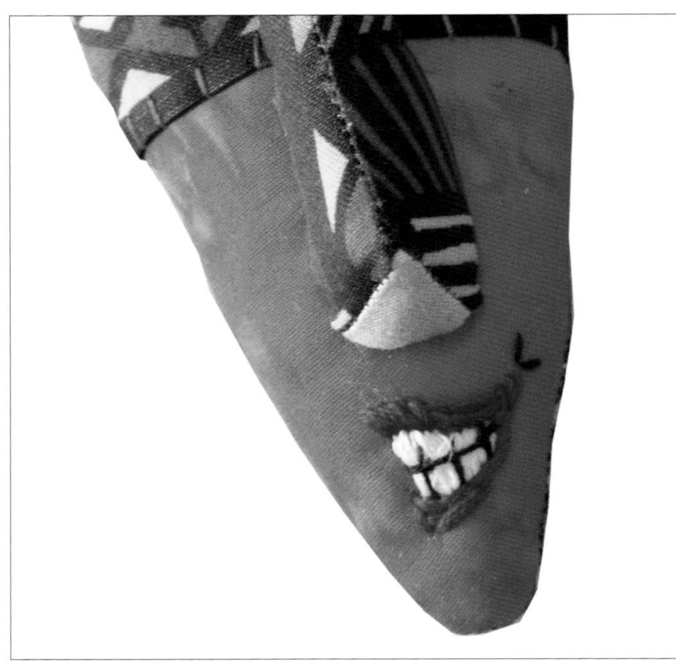

(f)
Build character with an unusual mouth shape.

Body

1. The body is a ball created by joining four identical shapes. With right sides together, match the triangles along one edge only of two body pieces. Stitch between the triangles.

2. Continue sewing the body pieces together at the sides. On the last side, leave a gap (g).

(g)
Join body shapes as shown.

(h)
Stuff the body firmly—or less so, for a more cuddly effect.

3. Turn the body through an opening and stuff it (h). Decide if you want a rigid or soft neck, and use the appropriate set of instructions, which follow.

Dowel Method for a Rigid Neck

1. Using a craft knife, carve a sharp point at one end of a 4" (10.2 cm) -long dowel. Using a twisting motion, push the dowel in to the head from the bottom of the stuffing hole (i). Remove the dowel. With a glue gun, put glue on the point of the dowel and in the hole in the head. Insert the dowel into the head.

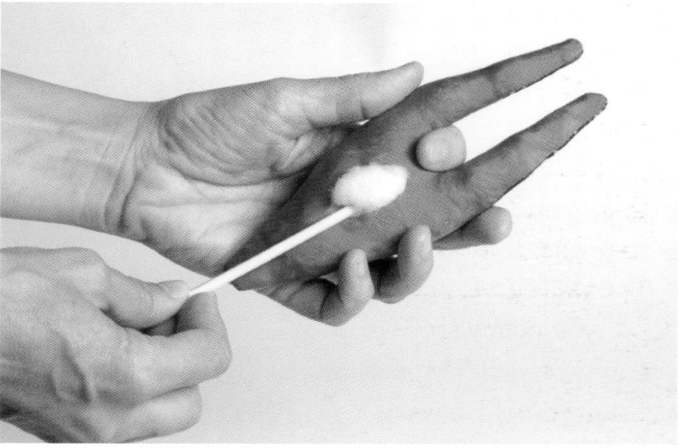

(i)
Insert a wood dowel to prevent a nodding Namba.

2. Sew the stuffing hole up around the dowel.

3. Paint the dowel, since it will be visible on the back of the finished doll.

Tip

You might want to insert some extra stuffing in the neck before you sew it closed. If it is the least bit weak, you may end up with a nodding Namba Teeke. For places you want to be strong and stiff without an external structure, try unscented, jumbo cotton balls. They are not good for large areas, as they tend to create a disturbing cellulite effect, but they are great for necks and the top of legs. Be careful to position the head just the way you want it, as this one is not moveable.

Simple Method for Attaching the Head to the Body

This method does not use a dowel in the neck or the head.

1. Firmly stuff the neck. Sew up the hole in the back of the head. Turn the ragged edge under and sew the neck shut.
2. Position the head in front of the neck so the chin touches the chest, and sew it to the neck.

Musings

Because the legs are going to be under the fringe, you can use any type of stitching you like. Experiment!

Attaching the Arms and Legs

1. Remove the stuffing from the top 1/4" (6 mm) of each arm. Choose one of the four sections as the front panel for the doll. Position the top of an arm to one side of the body. Pin the top of the arm, upside down, to the body. Stitch around the edge and across the top (j).

(j)
Attach the arms with a tab joint.

2. Attach the legs to the bottom of the doll using the same tab joint technique described for the arms.
3. Sew up the holes where you stuffed the arms and legs. Decoratively wrap fabric and yarn around each area. (This is a great way to hide a bad seam.)

The Puff

Fringe or ruffles can wrap Namba Teeke from head to foot, which is what makes this doll so voluptuous! You can shorten the puff process by using ready-made fringe or ruffles for your puff, or you can work from scratch.

If you opt to use the fabulous fringes awaiting you at your local fabric store, take your doll with you to help pick out the perfect color and length.

Alternatively, the instructions below explain how to make your own fringe swath using strips of tulle, eyelash yarn, and a very fluffy yarn. Do not stop at these suggestions. Use different colors and textures of yarn. You can make your doll's puff with fabric, plastic, beaded yarn, leather . . . whatever catches your fancy.

1. This step creates a fringe swath. Wrap a string around the Namba Teeke body to measure the doll's girth. Cut the tulle 4" (10.2 cm) longer than the doll's girth.
2. With both yarn ends held together and handled as one, wrap a few yards around all of your fingers. Feed at least 1" (2.5 cm) of a tulle strip into your sewing machine and start stitching down the center with a wide zigzag, then begin feeding the yarn off your hand (k). Continue feeding yarn off your hand while stitching it to the length of tulle.

Musings

Use different colors and textures of yarn for the fringe swath. I like to experiment with fabric, plastic, beaded yarn, and leather.

(k)
Sew one or two yarns to the tulle.

3. Measure the circumference of the doll's belly, midchest, and neck. Make a fringe swath for each measurement, again adding 4" (10.2 cm) to each measurement.
4. Starting low on the body so that the fringe will hang over the top of the legs, sew the longest fringe swath to the body. Add the next layer of fringe swath so it overlaps the sewing that attaches the previous fringe swath. Attach the final fringe swath around the neck.

Creativity Exercise:

Adventurer's Project: Gotcha Head

Draw the basic shape of the doll's face or photocopy the head pattern piece (page 114) and glue it in your book. Using the face or head as a reference—or working directly on it—play with colors and shapes, decorative elements, and textures. This can provide hours of fun as well as make the actual painting a quick, confident, and joyful experience.

1. Gather the Adventurer's Materials and Tools listed on page 26.
2. Apply gesso to the whole head with just one watery coat (two parts gesso to one part water) and let the head get very dry. This process and following steps will be easier if you place the head in a working mount (page 19).
3. Mush the paper clay around in your hands to loosen it up. Make two balls, each 1/4" (6 mm) across. Separately roll each ball to create little cylinders and tap the top and bottom to make each one flat. Poke a pupil hole in the middle of one end, for a faraway or doofy look. Set aside to dry.
4. Now roll a worm of paper clay and cut two equal pieces for the mouth. Press them into the face, leaving them in position, and set the work aside to dry.
5. Roll a 1/2" × 3/4" (1.3 × 1.9 cm) worm from the paper clay.

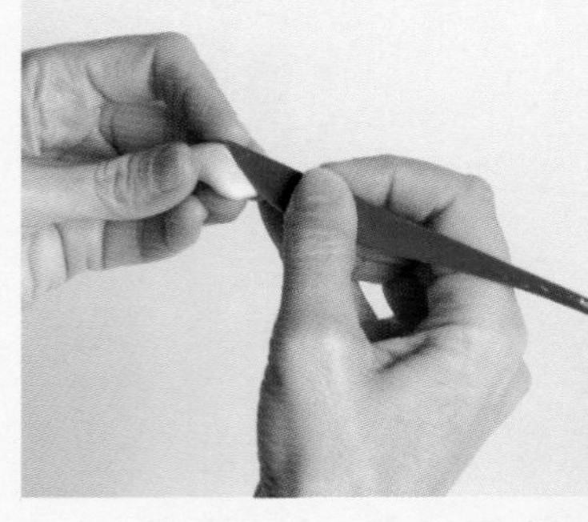

6. Flatten and hold the root. Bend the clay down. Flatten and round the tip.

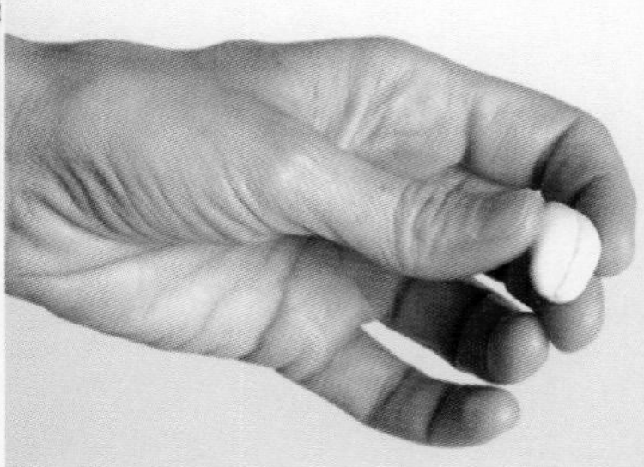

7. With a craft knife or the blunt side of an X-Acto blade, gently press into the middle of the tongue, to make a dent all of the way to the tip. Let the tongue dry.

How do you like this rather bug-eyed continence? It is amazing the different kinds of personalities that you can get in one little doll. This one is serious and traditional, much more like the inspiration for this doll, than its more doofy, personable counterpoint.

This might be a good time to follow Namba's example and get out your doll book (page 18).

8. For the snoot, lay a substantial paper clay worm down on the table, and use your craft knife to turn the length into a triangular roll. Press it in to the head where you want it and curve the top in between the ears. Remove the piece from the head and set it aside to dry.

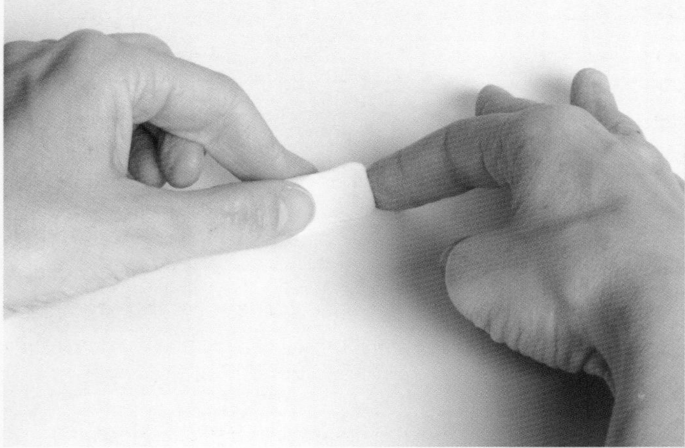

9. Once everything is dry, glue the features onto the head. Use your puff paints to make the raised decorations on the ears. Let everything dry again.

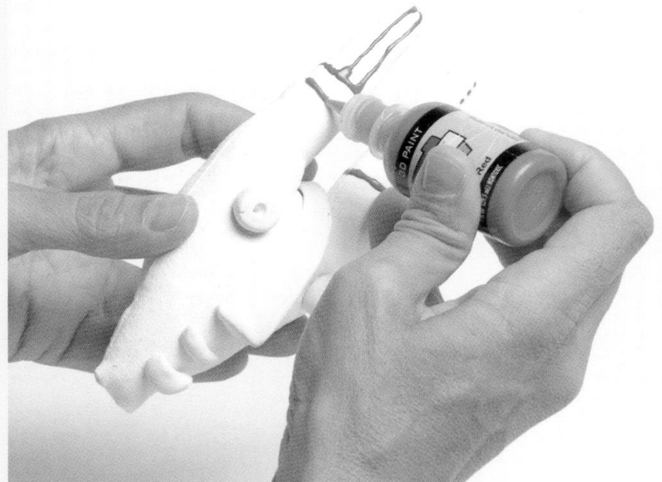

10. Cover the entire head with the Natural Sand Texture, let dry, apply gesso, and let it dry again.
11. Now the fun part! Paint the face to match the doll's body, or . . . not. Decorate the doll with beads and yarn or collage (page 102).

Gallery

QWAGGA, The African Striped Horse

Sue Farmer

The artist writes:

> As a child growing up in central Africa, I saw firsthand the African ceremonial garments with their dusty shading and stripped sisal leggings: grass fringing, cowrie shell trims, and found objects such as rusty nails and bottle caps. The coloring I favored was "hot Africa" with a limited palette. I also wanted to incorporate a current African trend—plastic bag recycling as art.
>
> After making up the original pattern in muslin, I revised the legs, rejoined them as one, and opted for the stump doll approach. The original body now becomes the base for the head. I chose to "corkscrew" the arm pattern and then bound it with bias-cut fabric. The horns or "ears" on the mask were altered to create a three-dimensional effect. The zebra stripe treatment, complete with mane, evolved quite naturally. African beads and a supply of rusty washers (sprayed with sealant) added interesting texture. Handmade turquoise polymer clay beads helped to break the repetitive color combination.

Ms. Namba Teeke Fruu Fru

Patti Medaris Culea

The artist writes:

> I can truly say that the project was a complete stretch for me. I typically create more traditional dolls, so this was a fun and exciting departure from fairies, finger turning, face painting, and sculpting.
>
> After creating the doll from white 100% cotton and changing the hand, I got out my stamps, Lumiere paints and Dye-Na-Flow dyes. Except for yellow, I selected colors I don't normally work with. After she was painted and dyed, I decided she needed a beaded head. I had taken a workshop with Annie Hesse and learned how to bead embroider a mask, so Ms. Namba Teeke got the works.
>
> The beaded mask was created using the head pattern without the horns. I dyed the cotton mask yellow then backed it with an iron-on stabilizer. I drew the design on the fabric and started beading. After the mask was complete, I hand sewed it to the head and then used an antique beaded fringe for her hair.
>
> Tyvek was painted using various colors of Lumiere paints. Once it was dry, I cut some for her skirt and some for her horns and arms. Other pieces were used to make the beads at her waist. An iron and embossing gun were used to create the curls and bubbles. Having been stretched to the limit, this was truly a fun doll and a visit to another world of doll making.

Cody Da Da

Cody Goodin

The artist writes:

> When I was asked to make this doll for Li's book I couldn't refuse. I have admired her work for a very long time. It also would present me with a creative challenge I had not had in a long time. The pattern was one of the most unusual I had ever seen.
>
> Namba Teeke would be my blank canvas. It took a few weeks of letting the spirit of the doll talk to me and tell me who it wanted to be. I tried out several ideas and then with a loud shout, it wanted to be made of leather and fur. I thought of the doll as a postindustrial sort of piece. The doll is constructed of recycled leather coats, fur, metal gears, ball chains, and bits of fibers and beads. Working with the leather was the most challenging part, as I had not used leather in this way before. I made the body out of the black leather from a recycled coat. Recycling is a big part of my doll-making experience, so it seemed appropriate that this doll be in that spirit. Behold my doll Cody Da Da.

Namba Teeke

Inez Brasch

The artist writes:

> Creating this Namba Teeke was a new experience for me because my work tends to be totally realistic and quite often monochromatic with very few embellishments. I've never, ever used a formal "doll book." I transfer ideas from my head to little scraps of paper or the backs of old, used envelopes. Sometimes I sketch out a whole figure, sometimes just the head. Since Namba Teeke is a pattern and shapes and sizes were already established, I concentrated on sketching out faces. The one I liked best had an African look.
>
> I wanted the fabrics and accent colors to reflect my concept of things African: earth tones accented by primary colors. Because I hate commercial doll stands, all my dolls are freestanding. Like all my others, this doll has an armature so the head can be turned; the arms can assume different poses and though it prefers to stand and will probably fight, could be made to sit. To ensure its standing, the bottom of the legs are weighted with lead shot.
>
> New experiences should teach us something. I learned that even when one has a pattern to go by, creating a doll book is a tremendous help. Having the fabric choices, accent colors, and surface designs all worked out in advance would be a lot faster and less frustrating than my "sit, stare, mumble incoherently, seat-of-the-pants" approach.

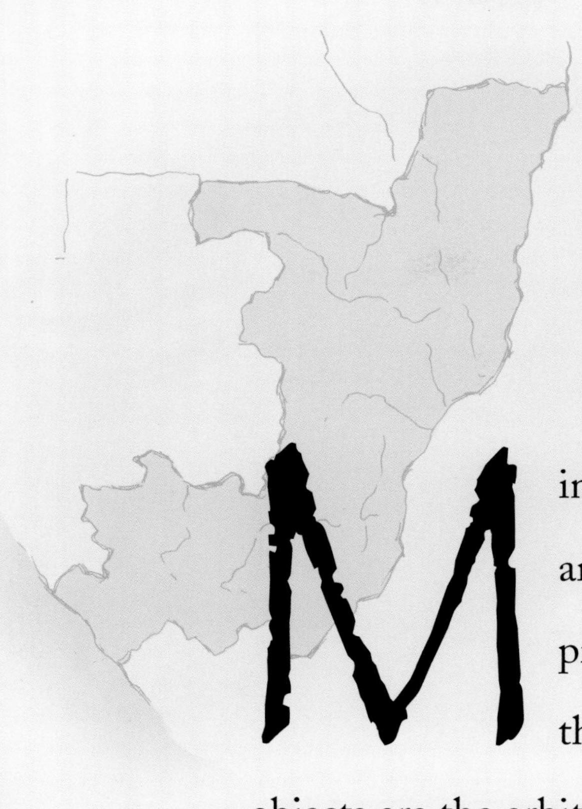

Minkondi (the plural of nkondi) are the intriguing and decidedly prickly figures that originate in the Congo and Zaire. These holy objects are the arbiters of the village, the ones that hold the people accountable to each other and to their world. Typically, they are carved by an artist who creates the personality that is revealed through the face and feet, as those are the only spaces that will not be eventually covered in nails.

Chapter 3: Healing

Kondi: Dancing in the Congo

A NKONDI IS EMBOLDENED WITH SPIRIT BY the nganga, the fetishist. A fetishist is much different than a witch doctor. A doctor is one who takes it upon himself to cast spells, to consort with the most dangerous and possibly evil of spirits, and intrudes in to other's lives with the intent to give one person power over another. He is not respected or revered but, instead, feared and avoided.

The fetishist, on the other hand, is the healer of the tribe, the one who restores universal harmony. He is asked to mediate between the other world and the members of the tribe on their behalf. He is the keeper of the village's nkondi. In a quite secret and mysterious ritual, he fills the cavity in the nkondi with magic (and herbs and medicines) and awakens the nkonde (the spirit of the nkondi) by touching it in a special spot left free of nails just for this purpose.

When there is a disagreement, or an agreement, the fetishist gathers the participants, awakens the nkonde, and as the agreement is made, he then licks the nail or spike and drives it in to the body of the nkondi to seal the pact. When the agreement is fulfilled, the nail can be removed. (It seems that this might be a bit tricky and perhaps is the reason so many wonderful minkondi remain with all of their nails in place.) This ritual is considered a binding contract and it is understood that if you break the contract, the nkondi could cause you all kinds of trouble. (In addition, everyone in the village would give you no end of grief over it as there was the nail right there, as tangible proof!)

The whole idea of recording agreements in this visceral, visual way delighted me, and I thought about it for quite a while. Finally, while doodling, the formidable grimace morphed into a raucous grin and Kondi was born!

Like our Kondi, a great many of the minkondi are dogs.

Materials

- basics, embellishing, painting and drawing, and sculpting kits (page 12)
- two fat quarters for the pattern pieces (Note: You can use a contrasting fat quarter for some of the pieces.)
- dense, low-loft cotton batting such as Warm and Natural Cotton Batting for the ears
- unscented cotton balls, heavyweight craft store felt, wool roving, or a steel wool pad for stuffing the body along the spine (Note: Test your fabric by poking it with a pin several times to be sure that the fabric will not leave gapping holes when pins are removed.)
- assortment of yarn in contrasting colors and textures for the neck ruff and front leg embellishment
- fringe for the neck ruff (optional)
- embroidery thread: white for the teeth and black for outlining
- matching sewing thread
- beading thread or strong cotton thread to match the eyeball fabric
- beads for the neck ruff (optional)
- light-color bead for each eyeball
- smaller, dark-color bead for each pupil
- puff paint
- masking or clear tape to join traced pattern piece shapes
- 9" (22.9 cm) -long 1/4" (6 mm) wood dowel, chopstick, or skewer for the neck

Tools

- pen with air- or water-soluble (disappearing) ink

Adventurer's Materials and Tools for Big-Grin Kondi Head

- fabric head temporarily mounted on a 1/4" (6 mm) wood dowel of any desired length
- fluffy yarn for the eyebrows
- acrylic craft or oil paint: white, yellow, luminescent white, ivory-black, red, and any desired color for the irises
- cylindrical object to roll paper clay flat

Adventurer's Materials and Tools for Agreements Book Screen

- two pieces of background fabric, both 8" × 10" (20.3 × 25.4 cm) for each panel
- fabric scraps for hinges, each piece no smaller than 3 1/2" × 6 1/2" (8.9 × 16.5 cm): three for each outside panel, six for each inside panel
- 7" × 9" (17.8 × 22.9 cm) of firm, double-sided (fusible on both sides) interfacing such as Dritz Heavyweight Inner-Fuse for each outside and inside panel
- acrylic paint in desired colors
- 11" (27.9 cm) of 1/4" (6 mm) dowel for every hinged edge (Note: Two panels share one hinge.)
- extruder (Note: This is a tube with a plunger and interchangeable tips, to create shaped clay tubes.)

Creativity Exercise:

Make a Fabric-Scrap Color Wheel

You know all of those scraps you just cannot part with? Use them to construct a fabric color wheel. I do this project whenever I have a great new idea for a doll but too many fabrics to choose from or am overwhelmed by a visit to my favorite fabric store. Seeing new combinations can open creative doors that were rusted shut just moments before.

1. Cut shapes of (predominately) red, yellow, blue, orange, green, and purple.
2. Choose a fabric for your backing (it can be made from anything you like). Cut the backing to 8" × 10" (20.3 × 25.4 cm).
3. Lay your scraps on the backing fabric so they resemble the basic wheel below. Sew or glue the scraps down and embellish them as desired. To sew down the scraps, randomly machine stitch over the surface, through all the layers.

You could use your fabric scrap color wheel as part of a book-screen backdrop for your Kondi doll (page 55 for instructions). It is just the right size.

Preparing the Pattern

1. Trace the pattern pieces (page 116) onto cardboard and cut them out. Tape the body gusset pieces together where noted to create a final pattern piece.

2. Trace the body, tail, ear (twice), front leg (twice), back leg (twice), and head on to the top layer of two pieces of fabric that are stacked right sides together. Cut the body and head from the fabric. Keeping the fabric layers together, set aside the remaining tracings.

3. Trace the joined body gusset and the head gusset on to a single-layer piece of fabric. Cut it out. Take a tiny V-shaped nick at the triangle on the body and at the split where you taped together the body gusset. The narrow part of the body gusset is the underbelly, centered on the taped "seam."

4. Choose one side of the body (a single body fabric piece) and line it up with the seam on the underbelly (a).

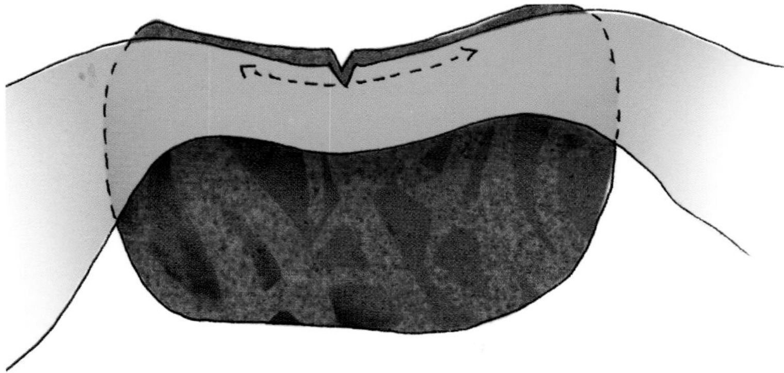

(a)
Start the assembly at the underbelly.

5. With the right sides together and working along a portion of the body gusset, start at the triangle and carefully sew around the body, almost to the end of that side of the body gusset. You want a loose seam allowance at the end of the gusset. Backstitch before you end. Go back to the triangle and go around the other way, to join the remaining (loose) part of the body gusset to the body, until you meet up with the first set of stitches.

6. In the same way, sew the remaining body piece to the opposite long edge of the body gusset (b).

(b)
Use two seams on each side of the body gusset to join the body pieces.

Musings

Play with your favorite colors for this doll. Consider making the body one color and the rest of your doll a contrasting color, or try making each pattern piece a different fabric. Use an interesting African fabric, or fur, or an old tablecloth, or some special scrap you have always wanted to turn into something!

7. Join the loose edges (the opposite ends of the gusset, which now meet) by sewing a little toward the center, say ½" (1.3 cm) or so, on both sides. Clip through the seam allowances almost to the seam line along the curved portions. Turn and stuff.

Stuffing the Body

The body is the *pin* part of the cushion, so it needs to be stiff. To stuff the body, place your felted swatch, silk, cotton batting, unscented cotton balls, or a wrapped steel wool pad inside the body, along the spine, where the needles will go in. Firmly fill the rest of the Kondi with polyester stuffing. Sew up the stuffing hole.

Tip

The traditional stuffing for pincushions—surprising to some—is human hair, but wool roving (unspun wool) or spun silk scraps will gracefully suffice, as will a nice piece of wool fabric that has been washed in very hot water several times. Cotton and wool yarn, packed tightly, also work and keeps your needles nimble.

The basic rule is that stuffing coming from anything other than the breathing and the walking (animals) will wreak havoc on your pin collection, especially if you live, like I do, in a location that has damp salt air.

That said, I have heard that plain steel wool pads are wonderful for keeping your needles dangerously sharp. Before inserting a steel wool pad in to the back of your Kondi, stitch it snugly into a pillow of tight-weave cotton, to keep the steel fibers from escaping.

Sewing and Stuffing the Legs

1. With right sides together, sew two back legs together along the traced lines, from dot to dot, up the leg. Do not sew across the bottom of the foot. Do not sew the thigh area. Do not sew the bottom of the foot. Cut out, leaving the seam allowance a bit wider around the thigh (rounded, upper portion of the back leg), to make it easier to turn under. Turn and stuff the leg area, leaving the thigh area empty and loose.

2. Situating the leg toward the back of one side of the body, place it so the stuffed part of the leg tucks under the body and the one-layer (outer) piece of thigh fabric extends on to the body back. Cut off the thigh flap that goes under the body, leaving just enough to cover the stuffing, and turn under to hide the exposed raw edge.

3. Carefully turn the edges of the thigh fabric under and pin (c).

(c)
Leg pinned to the body, shown upside down.

4. Use a ladder stitch (page 16) for an invisible seam to attach the thigh to the body. Leave about ½" (1.3 cm) open toward the back of the thigh, for stuffing. You can leave your needle and thread attached here while you stuff.

5. With your handy stuffing tool, poke some stuffing into the thigh area until you have a thigh shape (d). Sew up the hole.

6. Assemble, attach, and stuff the remaining back leg in the same way.

7. With the right sides together, sew two front legs together along the traced lines down the sides. Cut out, turn, and stuff firmly. Turn the top under and pin under the belly side toward the front. Sew it on.

8. Using a glue gun, place a small glop of glue inside the bottom of each leg and fold the raw edges in to close the feet. Decorate the legs now or when Kondi is finished (e).

(e)
Embellish the front legs with yarn and fabric fringe that is topped with beads.

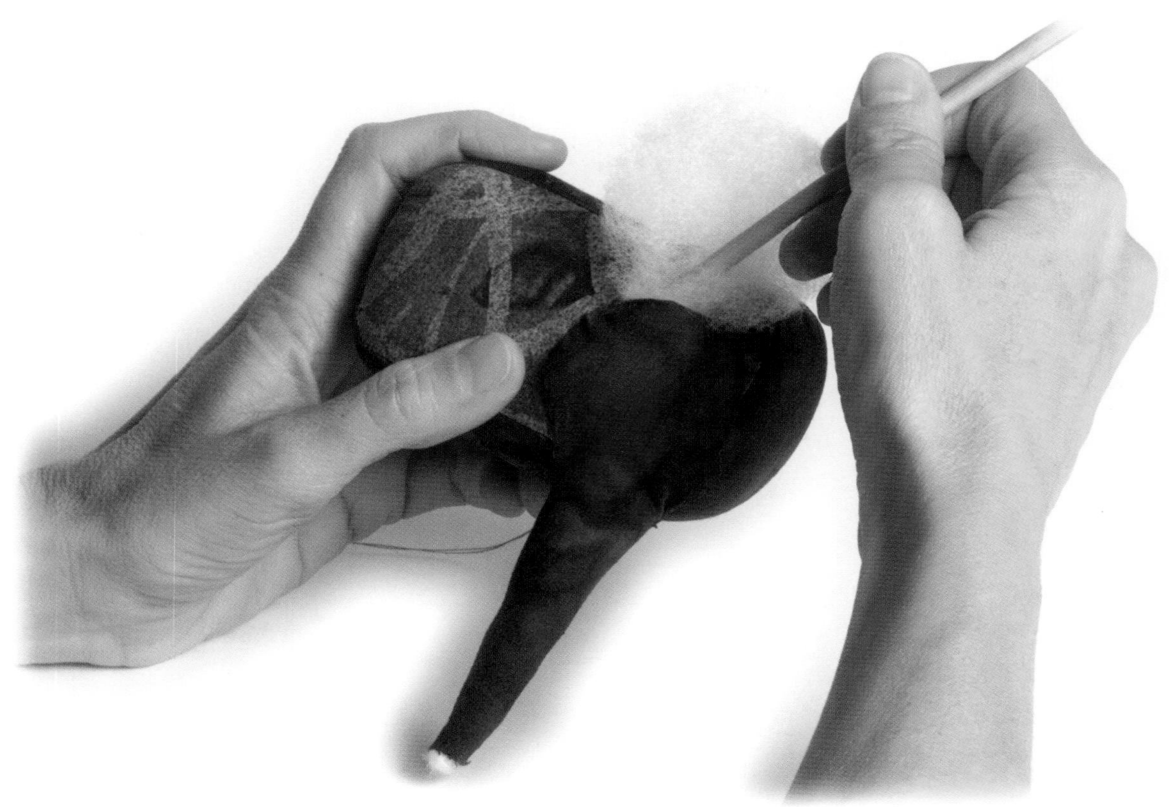

(d)
Stuff the thigh after sewing it to the body.

The Head

1. Sew the gusset to the head in the same way the body was attached to the body gusset, as follows: With one side of the head and the head gusset lined up at the triangles and with right sides together, sew around the head and gusset. Do this to both sides. Where the ends of the gusset meet, leave them open. Turn and stuff firmly.

2. With a craft knife, sharpen one end of the dowel to a point. Slowly twist the point into the head, through the stuffing hole. Decide how long you would like the neck to be, and make a mark where the neck and body meet (f). Remove the dowel from the head and body. Set aside the head. From the mark for the body, measure about 1" (2.5 cm) farther along the dowel. At the blunt end, create a point that is acute enough to puncture the fabric. Find the exact point from which you want the neck to spring from the body and puncture the body there. Slowly turn the dowel until it goes deep in to the body—this will make the head less likely to droop. Pull out the dowel, apply glue to the point and firmly push it into the body at the desired location (f).

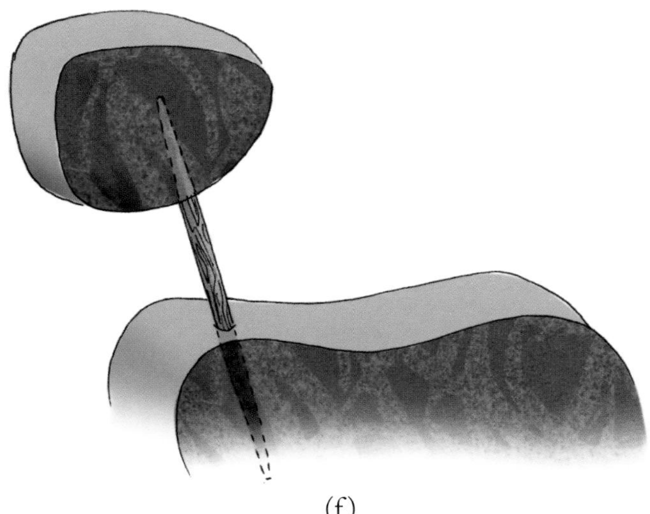

(f)
Insert the wood neck in to the body wherever you think it looks best.

3. Paint the neck, wrap it with fabric, encircle it with beads, or put a ruff around it (g). If you are interested in a ruff, get your store-bought fringe, lay the choice yarn morsels on top of the solid part of the fringe, and use a machine zigzag over the layers to join them. Then, starting from the bottom, lay down a bead of glue and wrap it up to the head.

The Ears

1. With the right sides of the fabric pieces still together, sew around the traced lines for each ear, leaving the bottom open (indicated on the pattern piece by dotted lines).

2. Turn and stuff the ears VERY LIGHTLY with the cotton batting. Turn under the bottom of the ear so that you have a clean end. Topstitch through both layers of each ear where the pattern says "stitch, stitch!"

3. Sew the bottom of the ears to the head.

(g)
Make a poofier ruff by closely wrapping the fringe.

Musings

Try a couple of positions for the ears. Ear position reveals the mood or personality of many four-legged creatures. If your Kondi is dodging the pins and needles of his reality, his ears might be laid flat; if he is curious, his ears may point in different directions. Check your resident four-legged family member for reference or make up an attitude of your own! If you want the ears to be perky, curve them a bit like a moon and stitch them on while maintaining this shape; they should stand right up.

The Tail

1. The tail is the thimble mount. With two fabric layers still right sides together, sew around the tail leaving the "butt-side" open. Cut around the tail. Turn it right side out and stuff firmly.
2. Sew the tail to the Kondi's buttocks.
3. Decorate with beads, fabric wrapping, and stamping, or with some collage work (page 102).

Needled Teeth

1. With a pen that has air- or water-soluble (disappearing) ink, or a contrasting-color pencil, directly on the head, draw the basic shape of a grin. Make it slightly smaller than you want it to be. You can use the mouth shown on the head pattern piece or in these sketches (h) as alternate grins.
2. Draw the basic horizontal line where the top and bottom teeth meet. With all six plies of a strand of white embroidery thread, stitch tightly up and

(h)
Study these drawings for ideas for your doggie.

down across the top, then along the bottom. Use satin stitch (page 17) or the long and short stitch (page 16) to fill in the entire mouth area. The idea is to get a really solid white space, so work the bottom teeth stitches up in to the top ones.

3. Using the pen with air- or water-soluble ink, VERY LIGHTLY make several dots where the teeth should meet. Using black embroidery thread, backstitch (page 14) or stem stitch (page 18) the line between the teeth.

4. With the thread, outline the teeth and outside of the mouth. This effectively hides any uneven stitching and makes the teeth really shine!

Eyes

1. With beading thread or strong cotton thread, make a tiny knot, bring your needle through the side of the face and up through the exact spot for an eyeball.

2. String a lighter bead, then the darker one, then go back through the lighter one (i). Insert the thread back in to the head at the same position, and pull it out at the position for the remaining eyeball. Stack the beads in the same manner, secure them to the head, and fasten off.

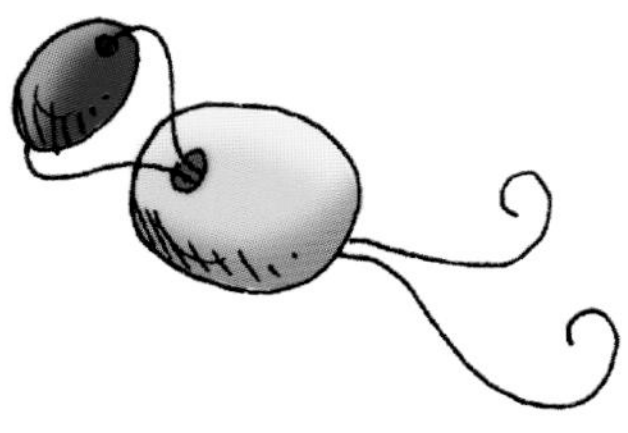

(i)
Sew a bead for each eye.

Creativity Exercise:

Adventurer's Project: Big-Grin Kondi Head

1. Gather the Adventurer's Materials and Tools on page 46.
2. Apply gesso to the head. Let it dry overnight.
3. Make two worms from paper clay, each about half as wide as you want your teeth to be tall. With a cylindrical object, roll them flat. One clay piece is for the top teeth and one is for the bottom teeth.
4. With a knife or clay tool, trim the edges to the desired shapes. Mark your teeth intervals by pressing lightly, just until you can see dents. Now smear glue on the back of the top and place these teeth on the head, where you would like them. Press and wait a bit. Do the same on the bottom.
5. Mold each tooth with deeper dents, rounding the biting side, and generally making them more dimensional. Let them dry.
6. After you are finished with the teeth, roll a very long paper clay worm and wrap it around the teeth like lips.

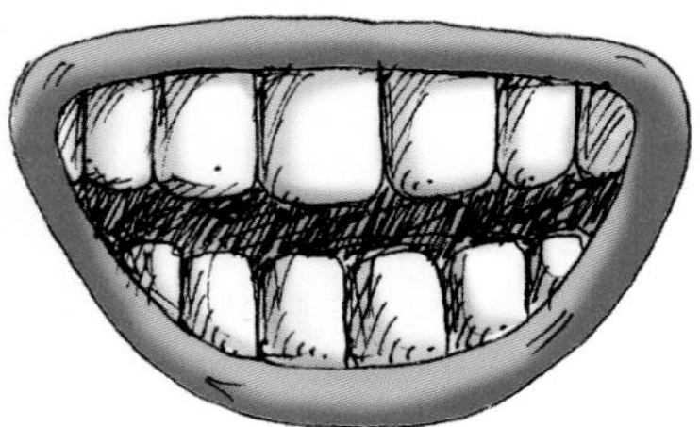

7. Glue the doll's lips to the face.
8. Roll two paper clay balls and squash them firmly on to the head where you want each eye to be positioned, to make two indents. Put white glue in to each indent. Gently press the balls in place. Hold them until they do not fall to the ground if you let go. Let all of this dry overnight or for most of a day.
9. Paint the whole face with gesso again. Let dry.
10. Paint the teeth white, add a tiny bit of light yellow as a wash over the entire surface, and then cover with luminescent white.
11. Paint the eyeballs with white, a yellow wash, and then luminescent white in the same way as the teeth. Then paint the irises and pupils.
12. Paint ivory-black in to the cracks between the teeth. Quickly wipe a cotton cloth over the teeth so they stay white and the black remains in the cracks and under the gums.
13. Paint the lips red.
14. Paint the base of the head to match the body or in a color that is in keeping with the character of your Kondi. If you are going to paint your little Kondi's body, do not paint the area where you will insert pins in the finished doggie.
15. Glue some fluffy yarn behind the eyeballs, for eyebrows.

Creativity Exercise:

Adventurer's Project: Agreements Book Screen

Tip

Ivory-black is made by many paint companies. It is more transparent than Mars Black, which would give your doll's teeth a malnourished, witchlike appearance.

What are your agreements with your family, the loves in your life, your world and how you move in it? What are the agreements you have with yourself? Just as a village nkondi is evidence of the agreements of people in a village, our culture is steeped in the agreements of our larger village . . . stoplights, taxes, clocks all set to the same time. All agreements, however small, are the minkondi of our world. What agreements in your life do you want to document? What magic can you hide in the pockets of this journal?

You can use paper for some pages (you can glue or sew on fabric hinges if you are careful), add a little book to one of the pages, insert a doll, or create a scene . . . the possibilities are endless.

Start this project by collecting the Adventurer's Materials and Tools on page 46.

Hinges

1. Cut a strip of fabric from scrap. The hinge sizes are just suggestions; you may choose to make them all the same, or some much larger or smaller. The only important guideline is that you need at least two hinges per side if you want the screen to stand up on its own. Here are some suggested dimensions:

- 2¼" × 6" (5.7 × 15.2 cm),
- 3½" × 6½" (8.9 × 16.5 cm), or
- 3" (7.6 cm) square

2. Fold the strip in half lengthwise. Sew the long edges together. Turn.
3. Cut the strip in thirds along the length.

Outside Panel

You can embellish your 8" × 10" (20.3 × 25.4 cm) pieces before, during, or after assembly. If you embellish before you assemble a panel, be sure everything you add can be ironed. Rocks, for example, wreak havoc on both an iron and ironing surface.

1. Start with an 8" × 10" (20.3 × 25.4 cm) piece of fabric face up on a table.
2. Lay the hinges on the fabric piece.
3. Remove every other hinge. Fold the hinges with the raw edges matching and pin them to a long edge of the fabric, with the ragged edges out.

4. Place a second 8" × 10" (20.3 × 25.4 cm) piece of fabric, facedown on top, sandwiching the hinges between the larger fabric pieces.
5. Sew down the hinge side.
6. Turn the sandwich right side out, with the hinges extending from the side of the panel.
7. Insert an interfacing piece between the large fabric pieces and push it against the hinge side, so the fabric is taut.
8. With the iron on high, press the sandwich until one side of the fabric is adhered. Take care you do not damage the embellishments or burn your fingers.
9. Turn over the piece and iron the second side.
10. Trim off the extra fabric around the sides.
11. Zigzag around all of the sides, and then work around them with another decorative or utility stitch. If desired, you can leave the hinge side without any topstitching.

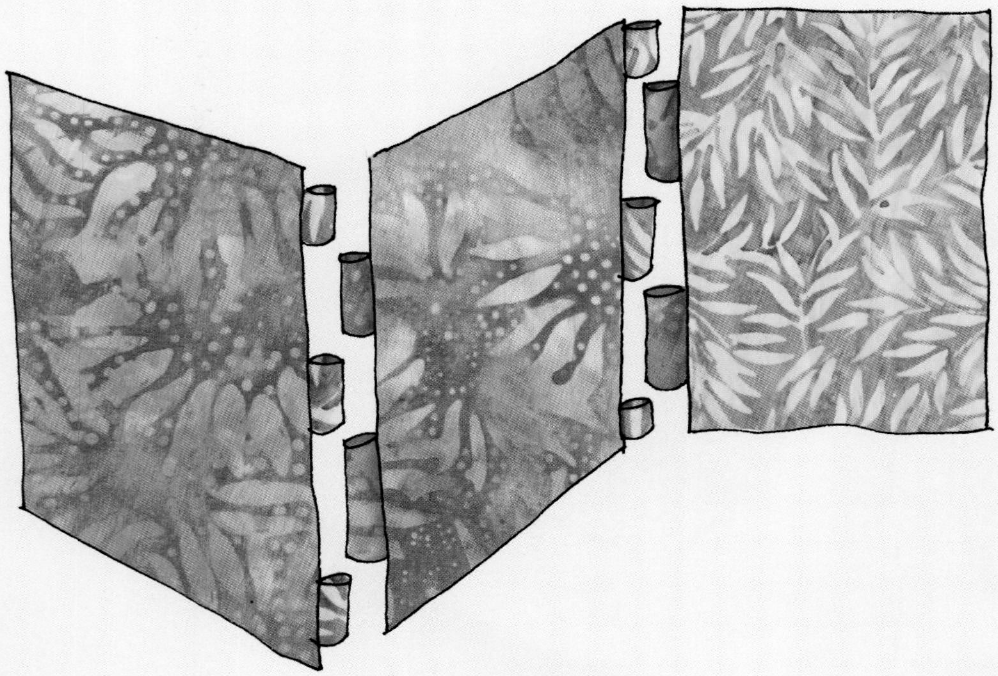

Inside Panel

When you make your second panel, you will want the first one handy so you can arrange the hinges properly. Overlapping edges have a bunchy effect that limits the ability of the screen to fold, and it looks like it has ruffles.

The middle panels are a bit different: There are hinges along both lengthwise edges. For these, create your sandwich by layering the materials in the following order, listed from bottom to top:

- 8" × 10" (20.3 × 25.4 cm) fabric piece, right side up
- hinges on both lengthwise edges, folded in half, with raw edges matching, facing out, and in position to alternate with the hinges on panels that will be on either side
- 8" × 10" (20.3 × 25.4 cm) fabric piece, facedown
- 7" × 9" (17.8 × 22.9 cm) double-sided interfacing

1. Zigzag down both of the long sides, very close to the edges of the interfacing. Trim the extra fabric off the sides.
2. Put your hand in between the two fabric pieces and turn the work right side out.
3. The interfacing is now between the two pieces of fabric. Iron to fuse the layers together.
4. Trim the extra fabric off the top and bottom.
5. Zigzag around all sides. Sew again with a decorative stitch, if desired.
6. Create as many panels as you want. Three is good if you want the work to stand up nicely.

Musings

If you want your book screen to stand up solidly, a foot on the bottom of each dowel is helpful. For each foot, make a spiral just like a finial. After the foot is painted, insert the dowel into the foot. If this is a book, make the foot removable. If this is a full-time screen, glue the foot in place.

Finials

Spiral toppers make your book extra special.

1. Roll (or use an extruder) to create a long worm of paper clay.

2. Draw a 1½" (3.8 cm) -wide circle on a piece of paper and lay the worm around the perimeter of the circle.

3. In an ever-decreasing spiral, lay the worm on top of itself to create a cone.

4. Add shapes to the spiral.

5. Fill the inside of the cone with paper clay.

6. Poke your dowel into the spiral until it is submerged at least ½" (1.3 cm). Remove. Let dry.

7. When everything is dry, paint the dowel and finial with gesso and acrylic paint.

8. Thread the dowels through the hinges.

9. Glue the finial on to the dowel. Tie or sew on fabric scraps as desired.

You are now officially a fetish maker, a healer, and in your hands is the power to re-establish universal harmony!

Nkondi

Rosie Rojas

The artist writes:

> I enlarged the pattern by 150%. I used only the body and chose dotted fabric to signify nails. I stitched and stuffed according to Li's instructions. I attached drilled legs using a teddy bear needle and carpet thread, stitching from one side to the opposite side, to make sure the legs were straight and held up the body. I attached a bedspring to the head using a large button to secure it, painted the eyes with white for the base, and chose black for the pupil. I glued the entire head and applied lightweight yarn. I attached a short thread cone to the tail area using carpet thread and covered it with the embroidery floss. I attached the head to the body by going through the button area all the way through the neck in to the body and shoulder areas. I then wrapped this in leather strips to hide unsightly thread and also to give Nkondi some glam.

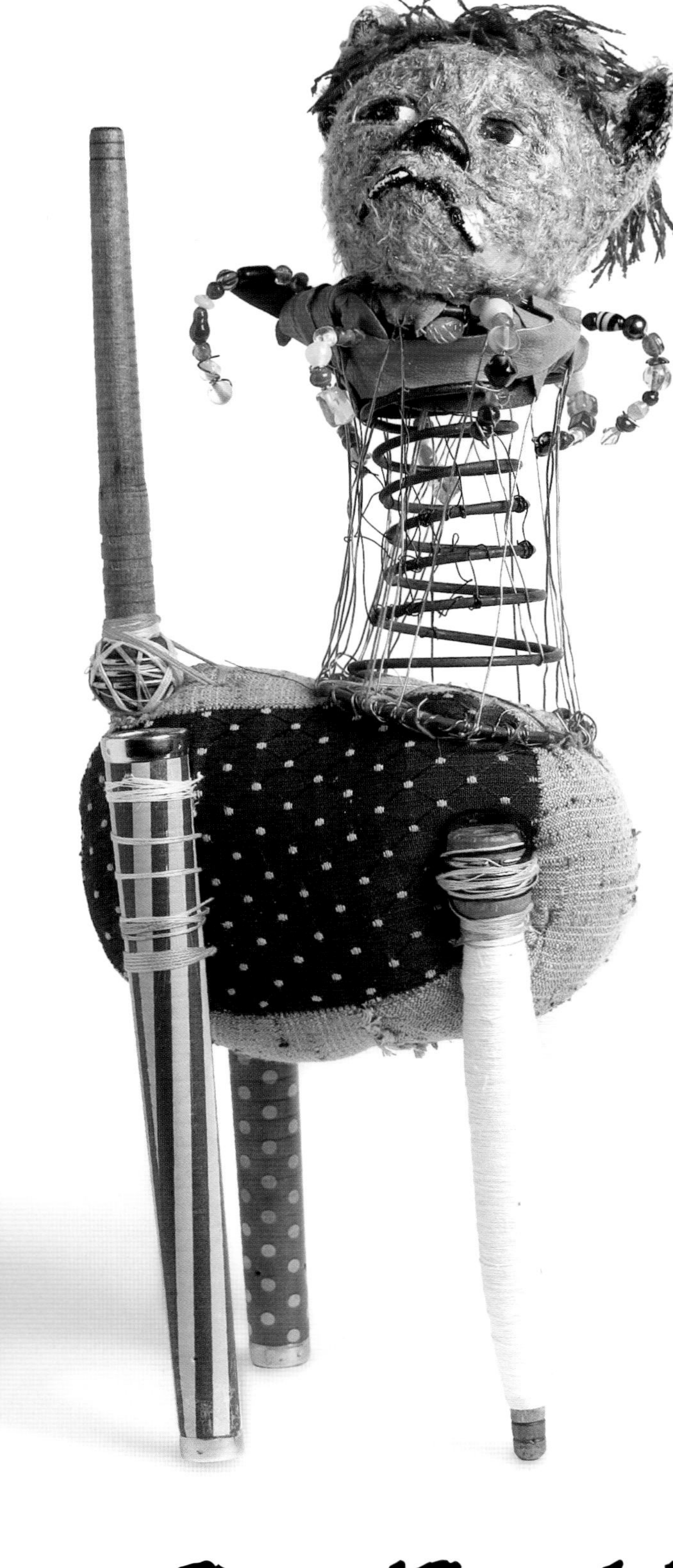

Gallery

McGukin: Bright and Common

Isabella Zambezi

The artist writes:

> McGukin is named after the King of Hardware Stores. He creeps through the aisles dropping helpful hardware hints all over your shoes and blowing the magic wood chips of inspiration into your ears.
>
> But he didn't start out so benevolent. I made the pattern in a truly horrid fabric thinking I would be able to use it as an exercise in creativity (sort of like picking your least favorite color and making a quilt infused with it, then falling in love with it). Unfortunately, everything around it withered, so bleak and oppressive was its heinous pattern and texture. In a dark mood, I slathered him in modeling paste, making a total mess, and felt much better. When he dried, I painted him with DecoArt No-Prep Metal Paint. If you ever have the need to evacuate a room quickly, open a bottle of this stuff. With burning eyes, I put him outside for the night. (Ventilate, ventilate, ventilate!)
>
> The next evening, I painted the eyes and mouth and used embossing powder to color my copper roofing nails. Then I wrapped them in colorful craft wire and poked them in to his body. I anchored the nails with glue from the gun and painted squiggles with 3D Crystal Color Lacquer around the nails. I added beads and yarn for decoration. The legs were originally as Li designed them but I thought the springs added a little zest!
>
> About the ATC: My Friend Martietta gave me a wool sweater that was really much too small . . . I cut it up and painted it with acrylic and nestled beads in to the crevices made by the cables. I squeezed an almost dry tube of puff paint in to stringy curls and finally used wire to attach two nails, each signifying an important agreement in my life.

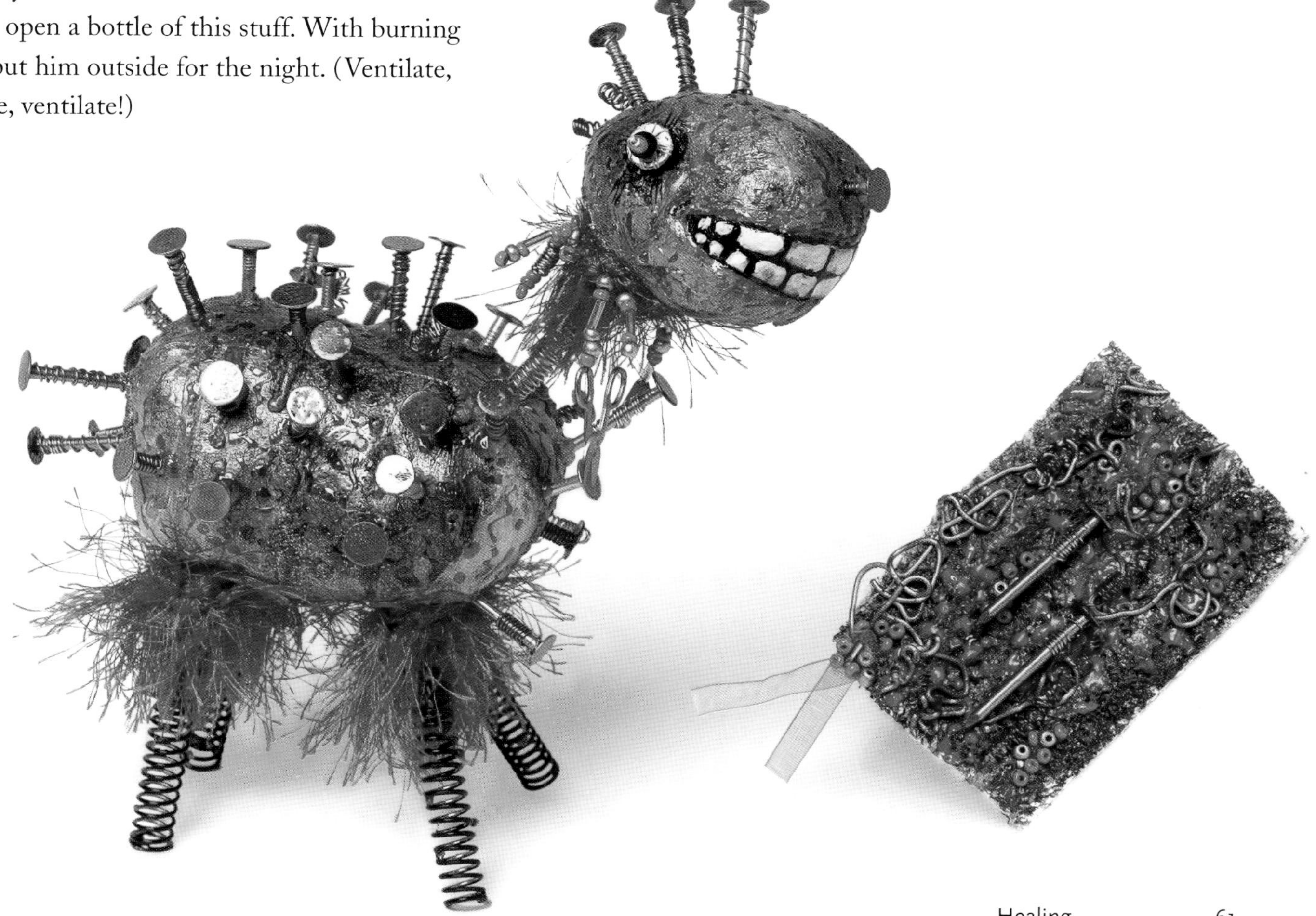

Wupatki means "tall house" in the Hopi language. The Wupatki National Monument is located 40 miles (64.4 km) northeast of Flagstaff, Arizona. Built more than 700 years ago, it is the largest pueblo of its time, and stands today as a monument to the meeting and merging of different cultures in a peaceful community.

Chapter 4: Magic

Wupatki: Touching the Earth

Ruins of Wupatki

THE SUNSET CRATER VOLCANO ABOUT 20 MILES (32.2 km) from the Wupatki ruins, erupted somewhere around 1064, forcing the Sinagua people who had been farming the area for centuries to find new homes. The volcano erupted and left thin layers of cinders and ash blanketing the land, providing a moisture-rich soil perfect for farming in the arid environment, and drawing many new tribes to the area. The Sinagua returned and were joined by the Winslow and Kayenta Anasazi, the Hohokam, the Hisatsinom, and another group known only as the "far wanderers." They shared the riches of the land and learned from each other while still maintaining their separate identities. The different cultures shared farming skills, traded pottery styles, and merged building techniques to create this "tall house" that still stands so regally today, many years later. Interestingly, there is no evidence of warfare in the ruins of these peoples. Somewhere in the 1200s everyone moved out. Why did this exodus happen? Did the spongy soil finally harden in the persistent sun? Did disease put them on the road? Whatever the reason, each culture was preserved and enhanced, and left a little richer. The merging of different beliefs and traditions created new ways of creating, thinking, and living. Many of the original clans and tribes are still in existence and claim ancestral and spiritual connection to Wupatki, revering it as a holy place.

This doll is named after that place and represents the themes of merging, magic, and storytelling.

He is reaching for the sky while grounded in the earth, washed in the past while pointing to the future.

Musings

Wupatki is a large site, blessed with many petroglyphs. Petroglyphs are images carved in rock, usually by prehistoric, especially Neolithic, peoples. They were an important form of pre-writing symbols, used in communication from approximately 10,000 B.C.E. to modern times, depending on culture and location. This one is said to be evidence that in the beginning we, like the sacred lizards that guard the gates of the ancestors, had long tails. What about adding a tail to your Wupatki?

The flute player shown below is found at Wupatki etched in the sandstone and might be mistaken for a Kokopelli. But if you asked a Hopi you would find that the deity portrayed is actually the flute player, Lahlanhoya. Kokopelli is the randy Katchina who sneaks into the dances and chases girls around trying to catch them with the end of his cane, the quintessential dirty old man. Lahlanhoya is the mark left by the flute clan; he is the trailblazer, the one who marks and commemorates the travels of the tribe.

Flute player from Wupatki.

Not all flute players look alike. This Lahlanhoya is from the Petrified Forest National Park.

Musings

The Hopi people who claim at least eight family clans originating from Wupatki call the ancestors Hisatsinom, "the people of the past." The Dine (Navajo) who occupied the area in the 1800s, use the word Anasazi for "the ancient ones" or more darkly noted, "the ancient enemies." The Pima use the word Hohokam for the more nebulous meaning "those who have left."

Materials

- basics, embellishing, painting and drawing, and sculpting kits (page 12)
- two fat quarters of contrasting fabrics for the unpainted version
- 1/8 yard (0.11 m) muslin or tight-weave cloth for the painted version
- few feet (about 0.5 m) of one or more yarns and fabric strips for the hat
- strong matching thread, or embroidery thread for attaching body parts
- 7" (17.8 cm) square of card stock for the hat
- Liquitex Modeling Paste for the painted version
- fine sand for mixing (optional) in to the modeling paste for the painted version
- two 10" (25.4 cm) lengths of 1/4" (6 mm) dowel for the body
- manufactured base or interesting piece of wood or other material at least 5 1/2" (14 cm) square for the base (Note: The base must be stable and you need to be able to drill in to it.)
- erasable pencil for the base
- masking or transparent tape to join traced pattern piece shapes
- finished artist trading card (page 76) (optional)

Tools

- erasable pencil
- tool for spreading modeling paste for the painted version
- pointed tool for incising for the painted version
- acrylic paint in colors desired for the painted version and the hat
- ivory-black acrylic paint for the painted version
- puff paint
- container to mix gesso and water for the painted version
- electric or hand drill and 1/4" (6 mm) bit for the base
- access to a photocopier for the petroglyphs painting (optional)

Adventurer's Materials and Tools for Dancing Spirit Headdresses

- two to seven yarns or fabric strips, each 12" (30.5 cm) long for the Pipe-Cleaner Plumage
- acrylic paint in colors desired for the Shaman Headdress
- two pipe cleaners for the Pipe-Cleaner Plumage
- paper clay such as Creative Paperclay or Delight Modeling Compound for the Shaman Headdress
- 18-gauge galvanized steel wire for the Shaman Headdress
- wire snips for the Shaman Headdress

Wupatki Body

There is a very basic version for Wupatki, with both arms raised, and readied with dowels that you can put in to a base. You can also make him with one arm outstretched, like the painted version shown to the right.

There are instructions for painting your doll on page 73 and for changing the arm position on page 69. Whatever your choices, start with the instructions here.

1. Trace the pattern pieces (pages 117–119)—except the headdresses and hat—on cardboard and cut them out. Tape the torso to the lower body and legs where noted. For a single raised arm, trace the dashed line on the doll's right shoulder. This effectively removes the right arm. The replacement arm is a separate pattern piece. Trace this Outstretched Arm on to cardboard and cut it out.
2. If you plan to paint your doll, use the muslin fabric. If you are making the unpainted version, use the fat quarters. Lay fabric right sides together and trace the taped body and two thumbs, on to the fabric. If only one arm will be raised, also trace the outstretched arm. Do not cut out a headdress yet.

3. Sew around the traced pattern pieces through both fabric layers, leaving open only the outstretched arm where indicated. As you sew around the fingers, it is important to backstitch at least once between each finger.
4. Cut out all the traced and sewn pieces.
5. Make a vertical slice in the middle of the front of the body and turn.
6. Stuff the head and hands firmly.
7. Wet the top of a dowel and roll a thick swath of stuffing around it. Insert the dowel, fuzzy end first, in to a leg until only the last 5" (12.7 cm) of the dowel is visible. Repeat this step with the remaining dowel and empty leg.
8. Hold the dowels toward the center and stuff around them with a slender stuffing tool, pushing stuffing into the legs, first on one side and then the other. Ensure there is stuffing all around both dowels (a). This will anchor them in to the body so Wupatki will not droop in the middle when he is placed in the base.
9. Finish stuffing the doll firmly. Sew up the hole.
10. You can make an outstretched arm bendable (at right). You must add the lever before the attaching the arm. If your doll has an outstretched arm, sew it to the body.

(a)
Hold the dowels together as you stuff the body.

Creativity Exercise:

Bendable Arm with an Internal Lever

One of the wonderful things about working in fabric is its malleability. If you would like an outstretched arm to bend, make an internal lever that will function much like your own muscles and tendons.

1. Bend the arm as desired. On the inside of the arm, pull a needle and thread through 1/2" (1.3 cm) above the elbow bend. Tie a knot. Go back in to the arm and come out the other side of the elbow. Go back in to the arm and come out the other side of the bend and pull. This will anchor the curve.

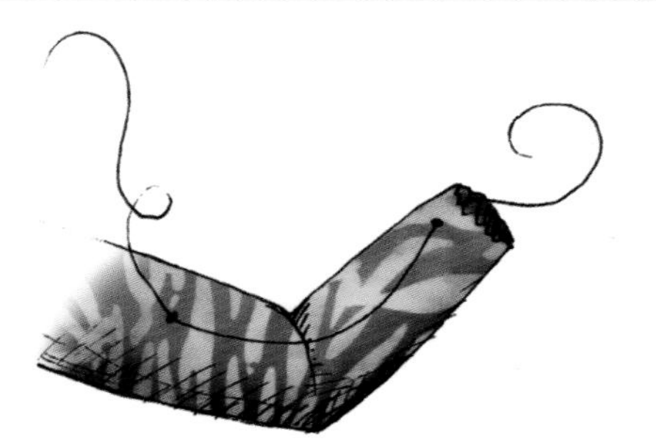

2. With a dull stuffing tool, push into the curve. This will make a single, deep fold.
3. Sew along the fold.

Base

1. Position your doll on top of the base where you would like him to stand. With an erasable pencil, draw around the base of the dowels.
2. Carefully drill through the base where you have marked.
3. Insert the dowels into the holes to make sure they are deep enough. It is really fun to complete the base now so you can use it throughout the doll-making process. But do not glue the doll into the base until both are complete.

Thumbs

With both hands raised, Wupatki's thumbs would most logically both be on the head side of the hands (check this out with your own hands). You can, of course, turn the hands out if that seems like something he may be doing.

1. Lay the thumbs, still wrong side out, on the hands, as you would like them to be, pencil an X on the side facing the hand. This will ensure that you have two DIFFERENT thumbs.
2. Make a slit on the side of each thumb that has the X and turn both right side out.
3. Stuff the thumbs firmly and the round part lightly.
4. Attach a thumb to each hand by hand sewing around the round part (b). As you work, add a little more stuffing to poof up the palm a bit.

(b)

Headdress

For different head ornamentation options for your Wupatki, skip this step and see Dancing Spirit Headdresses (at right).

1. Chose a headdress pattern (page 119).
2. With two fabric pieces right sides together, trace and then sew around the shape, leaving the bottom open where noted on the pattern. Turn and stuff.
3. Pin the headdress in several locations. Once you find the sweet spot, sew it on.

Creativity Exercise:

Adventurer's Project: Dancing Spirit Headdress

Gather the Adventurer's Materials and Tools on page 68 and then make your headdress of choice according to the instructions that follow. After it is painted and dry, poke the headdress wire deep in to the head and secure with hot glue.

Shaman Headdress

1. Form the paper clay into the shape you desire.
2. With your wire snips, cut a 1½" (3.8 cm) piece of wire, make a small curlicue in the top, and poke the curlicue side in to your shape. Squeeze the clay together so the wire extends out of the base of the shape, where it will attach to the head. Let dry.

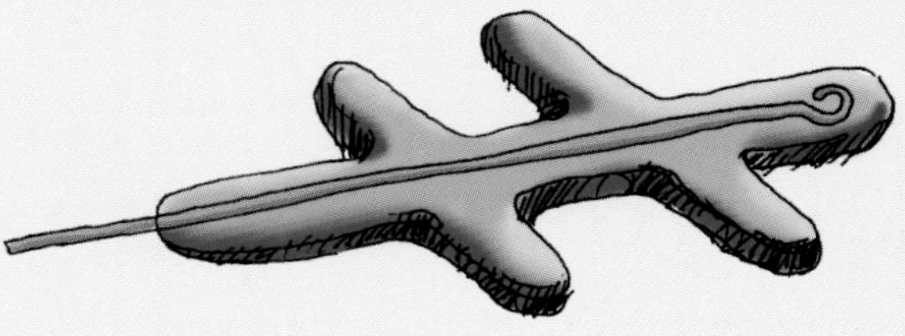

3. Apply gesso, let dry, and paint.

Pipe-Cleaner Plumage

Wrapping pipe cleaners is a very easy process, adds a bendable object to your arsenal, and can easily attach to virtually anything. Start with a new pipe cleaner. Bend one end around the widest yarn or fabric and, emulating the motion of a barbershop pole, twirl the yarn around the pipe cleaner to cover it. Do this as many times as you need to create a multicolored, multitextured, infinitely bendable headdress.

(c)

Petroglyph Key

1. Warrior, honest
2. Regenerate
3. Friendship
4. Moon, night
5. Lightning, storm
6. Stars
7. Clouds
8. Solstice, woman, water
9. Rain, storm
10. Hogan, home
11. Running water, constant life
12. Sun, new life
13. Shaman, wise, watchful
14. Rainbow
15. Bird's feet
16. Sun, awake
17. Go this way
18. Man, self
19. North star
20. Found
21. Strong medicine
22. Discussion
23. Hill, mountain
24. Here, this place
25. Look this way
26. Sacred site
27. Waves, river
28. Trail

Painting Wupatki

1. Paint a light coat of gesso over the whole body, being careful to smoosh it into all of the crevices. Let dry.

Tip

There is a lot of drying in this process. If you are like me, absolutely not able to wait overnight to finish things, you might want to have a heat gun handy. A hot lamp or hair dryer works equally well.

2. While drying the doll, play with your designs. Photocopy the doodle blank template (it will fit handily into a 5½" × 8½" [14 × 21.6 cm] sketchbook) (page 119) or draw your own. The marks you incise in to your doll will look carved. What do you want to carve in to this world? How does this doll inspire you to express, what does he call out for? Does he call for symbols of his own or would they be inspirational. Note traditional symbols and the cultures they come from (c).

Panther Shaman

Monster Slayer Petroglyph

Water Ghost Woman

Musings

Many petroglyphs are faceless. This is absolutely an option here: leaving a void to be filled by each different viewer is a rich and enticing experience. But if your Wupatki shakes his head and rolls his bulgy eyes at the thought of going faceless (like the Panther Shaman of the Ute at left), consider the eyes of this New Mexico Navajo Dinetah rock art of the all-powerful Monster Slayer, or perhaps the none-too-happy-looking Water Ghost Woman of the Dinwoody Tradition in Ancient Wyoming. But in my opinion, the very best rock art faces come from Down Under. The Wandjinas of the Kimberleys region of western Australia who bring rain, babies, food, and bounty, have big round eyes and long, straight noses. Look at the Wandjina drawing. They have no mouths because if they did, it would always be raining and as you know too much of a good thing can be . . . well . . . in this case, a flood. Sketch faces, play with the size and shape of the features, and be sure not to take their placement for granted ... experiment!

Wandjina

3. Mix two parts gesso and one part modeling paste. Apply this liberally everywhere you want texture. Mix sand in to the solution if you would like a gritty, rocky surface.

4. With a pointed tool, incise patterns on the body (d). You will get little buildups here and there, so scoop them up and redraw the line. If you make a "mistake" just smooth it out and begin again. This is a very forgiving medium. Let dry.

5. Add puff paint for a sculptural effect. Do the same to the base. Let dry.

6. Paint both the base and the doll one last time with gesso. Let dry.

7. Paint the background colors. Let dry.

8. Water down some ivory-black and paint it on a small portion. Rub a cotton cloth in to the crevices. Wait a minute. Now wet the cloth and rub on the places you want to really shine through with a more pure color (e).

9. Paint and collage (page 102) over the wiping to lighten, clarify, and brighten.

10. Attach an artist trading card to the front of the Wupatki (page 76).

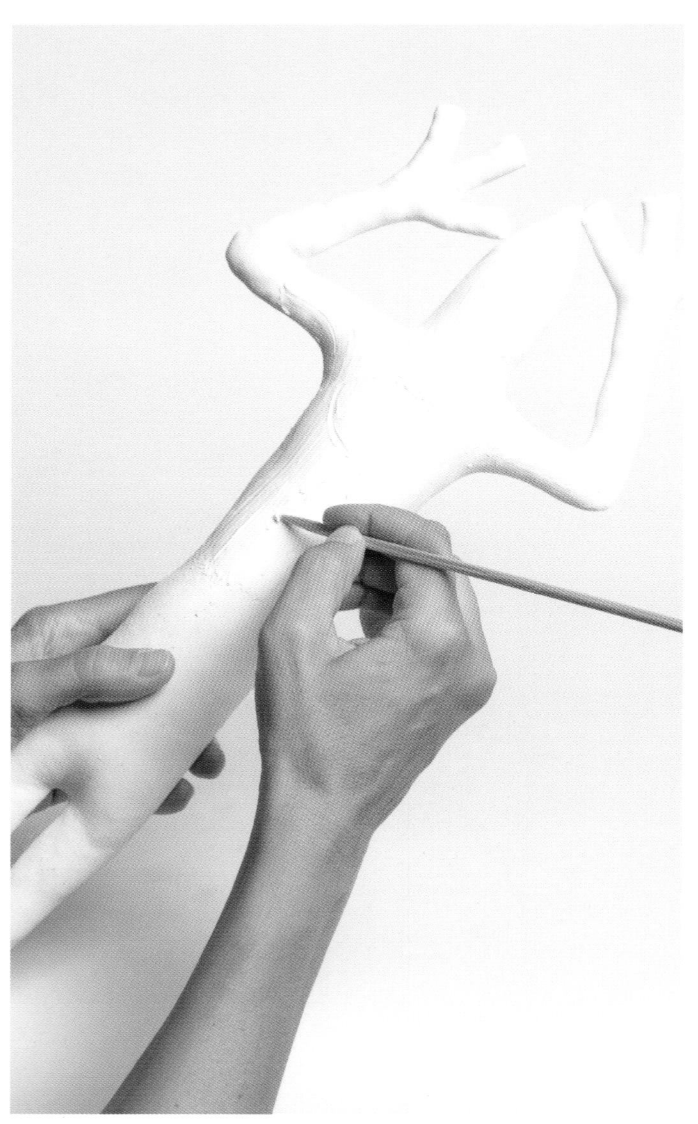

(d)
Incise patterns in the gesso-paste coating.

(e)
Rub ivory-black in the crevices.

A hat of eagle feathers;
A hat of eagle feathers,
A head-dress was made for me
That made my heart grow stronger.

—Excerpt from Pima coyote song

A hat, the correct hat, that perfect hat, can make your heart grow stronger!

The Hat

1. Paint the card stock you are going to use for the hat. Using the pattern (page 117), trace the outline and cut it out.

2. Bend and tape the card stock into a cone, leaving a little hole at the top. Collage (page 102), if desired.

3. Cut three or four yarn strands to 4" (10.2 cm) long and twist them together. Knot one end. From the inside of the hat, push the strands through to the outside through the opening at the top.

4. Squirt a sizeable blob of glue into the inside of the top of the hat to secure the yarn topknot.

5. Add some yarn on the sides and back around the edge of the hat, attaching it with the glue gun to the inside of the hat.

6. Glue the hat firmly on Waputki's head if you want it to be permanent.

Creativity Exercise:

A Wupatki ATC

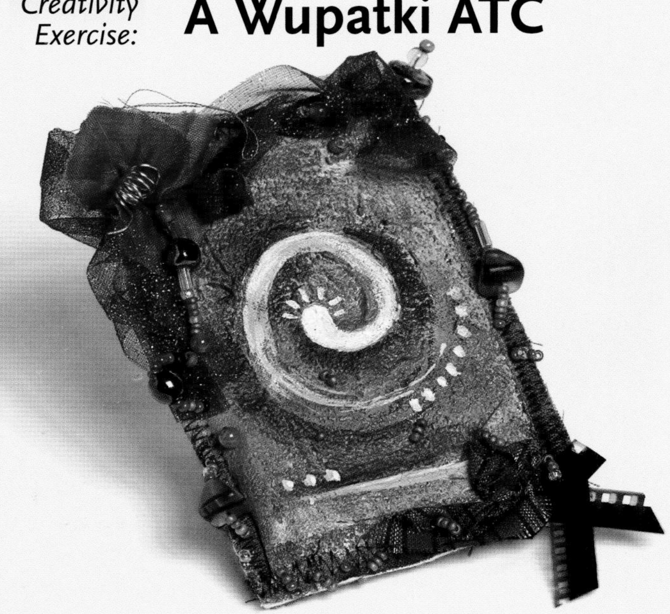

Timeless symbols and scratches leave messages both complex and simple, visceral and ordinary.

Artist trading cards (commonly called ATCs) are miniature works of art. They are a relatively recent invention and everyone is making them: stampers and scrapbookers; painters and sketchers, fiber artists and quilters, cartoonists, very, very serious folk, and us! The cards are 2½" × 3½" (6.4 × 8.9 cm), the size of a playing card, and are created to share and to trade. They are made from fabric or paper and are mounted on a sturdy paper or a double layer of dense, low-loft batting. The back side typically includes the name of the artist, the date completed, a signature, and the number if they are created as part of a limited edition. Everything is fair game, but if you are trading with a group that uses baseball card trade books in which to collect the cards, you will need to consider the altitude of your art. (A ½" [1.3 cm] bead will not allow the card to fit in to the pocket.) If that's not a concern, go sculptural!

If you are placing an ATC in the pocket on the front of your doll, of course consider the doll and the ATC in one circle of thought—make the ATC speak for your Wupatki.

If you would like to try an "on-the-wall" petroglyph ATC, follow the simple instructions at right. Or, if you would like to go off on a delightful tangent all your own, check out the ATC prompts on page 78.

Creating an Etched Petroglyph ATC

This ATC is inspired by the symbolic language of rock carvings, the ancient messages of the petroglyphs. They seem so permanent, still telling stories today: "saw two deer this morning" or "we lost the battle and our souls will now be the river."

Here is how to make a simple ATC with a rocky message.

- Choose a symbol from the chart on page 74 or make your own.
- Cut fabric to 3" × 4" (7.6 × 10.2 cm).
- Mix sand, gesso, and some Liquitex Modeling Paste. Apply it to the fabric.
- Using a sharp tool, incise a symbol in to the mixture. Let dry.

- Paint with gesso. Let dry.
- Paint with acrylic in the desired colors. Let dry.
- Cut to 2½" × 3" (6.4 × 7.6 cm).
- Machine zigzag stitch around the edges.
- Add beads, embroidery, and other embellishments (sand, gesso, and modeling paste lay waste to needles in seconds—use an old needle!).

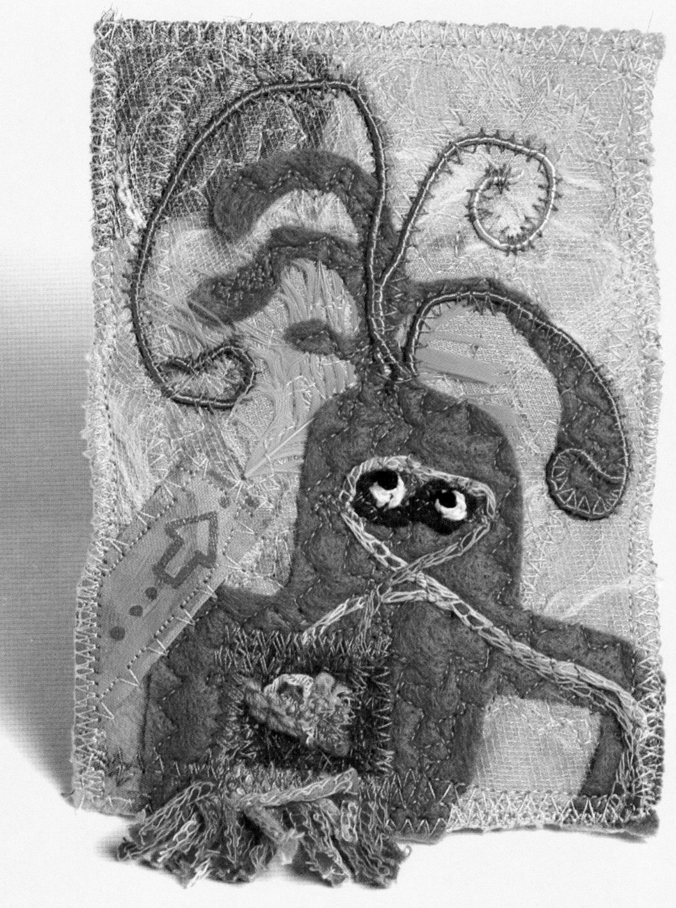

Creating a Layered-Fabric ATC

Sketch the Wupatki on to a page in your sketchbook with a lead or light-color pencil. Using a new color, extend the shapes, elongate the arms, pinch the top of the head into a fountainesque spiral, shorten the legs, and continue to play with this figure until you create an exciting new form.

1. Once you have the basic shape, cut it out of base fabric cut a little larger than 2½" × 3" (6.4 × 7.6 cm).
2. Place choice morsels of yarn, fabric, and ribbon strategically around and over the shape.
3. Cover with a layer of tulle.
4. Machine topstitch through all layers, over and around the scattered morsels, being sure to secure all pieces.
5. Cut a background cotton fabric to the same size as the ATC.
6. Cut a piece of dense, low-loft batting, such as Warm and Natural Cotton Batting, to 2½" × 3" (6.4 × 7.6 cm).
7. Hand tack the batting to the back of the backing fabric with a couple of loose stitches.
8. Add the collaged layer to the backing, right sides together. The batting is on the bottom.

9. Sew around the rectangle using a ¼" (6 mm) seam allowance and leaving a shorter side open.
10. Turn and press. Turn under the edges of the open side, and iron.
11. Zigzag around the whole thing with a tight stitch to make a solid border.
12. Embellish to your heart's content!
13. Use a Sharpie to sign the back with the date, the name of the ATC, the number in the series, and your name.

ATC Prompts

A petroglyph is a very simplified drawing. It distills an idea to its essence. What is your essence? One way to approach this is to take a picture of yourself, draw an outline, then fill it in. This solid shape is your petroglyph. Now, pretend as if this shape were soft clay, and pull, push, and play to create a different shape. Pull the essence out, make a hunter, create a monster or angel. Create a petroglyph of you. Write the name of your petroglyph and use symbols to describe it.

- Make up a language of scratches and dots, write something important, and send the ATC to a stranger.
- Count up things you want to tell people. The need to record our life is a universal, visceral need. Wupatki's friends and neighbors used rock carving and painting to say, "Look! I killed five, count 'em FIVE, mastodons! Oh wow! Look at me!" or "These are the things I know, this is what means something to me: this, and this, and this!" Find something to tell everyone. With simple marks, tell it.
- Use felt to make a soft wall and lay yarn pieces on top in a telling pattern. Using a felting needle, merge the yarn in to the felt background.

For a Namba Teeke–inspired ATC

- Create a mask to hide behind.
- Create a mask to show off your real self.
- Find a wonderful African fabric. Use it to create an ATC. With grommets, add legs, arms, and a head to the ATC, so your card can shake its head and swing its legs.

For a Kondi-inspired ATC

- Use some screen as the base, bend it (be careful not to cut your fingers!), stitch it, paint it, and weave your agreements in to the mesh.
- Create an ATC out of a piece of wood. Hammer a big nail into it, and then decorate the nail.
- Find the landscape that your Namba lives in, create an ATC from the colors of that landscape, and give it a name.

For a Goddess-Inspired ATC

- Draw the goddess/god in you and add wings.
- Find a piece of printed fabric you love, cut a small piece, and glue it in to the middle of a piece of ATC-sized matboard. Extend the pattern by drawing or painting it beyond the piece of fabric. Morph the pattern into something different by the time it gets to the edge.
- Cut out the shape of a kimono. Decorate it with beads and stitching. Fold the arms in and put a secret message under one sleeve.
- Use an old photo of something you love, dig up all your old buttons, discarded trinkets, and tassels, and then frame the beloved image with jewels!

Attaching the ATC

Choose your favorite ATC and decide how you are going to attach it. If you would like to house it in a nice window of plastic, follow the instructions below. Remember that plastic melts pretty easily and can smell like the equivalent of burning hair and really old tuna casserole. Test, test, test!

1. Cut a plastic rectangle to the size of the ATC, plus a 1/4" (6 mm) seam allowance around the whole card. If your ATC is dimensional, make the sleeve larger.
2. Hot-glue, sew with blanket stitches (page 15), or pin (use four) the plastic sleeve to the doll on three sides, leaving the top open.
3. Slip the ATC in to the plastic sleeve.

Musings

Have you embellished to your heart's content? Have you sewn on unusual things? Have you glued, taped, screwed, and somehow affixed the perfect things into place? ATCs offer the perfect format for experimentation and play. Have fun making one, or several, to accompany your doll projects.

Gallery

Guardian and Mojo

Kathy Kenny

The artist writes:

> I had fun playing with this pattern. I took it in a personal direction, using the form and the shape to play up my love of bags and talisman.
>
> The first doll, Guardian, is the beginning of morphing the pattern into a personal power symbol. She's still recognizable, yet has already lost the petroglyph feel. I laughed out loud when I realized I could allow her to hold a secret thought!
>
> Mojo, the green bag/doll, turns the raised-arm doll into a bag that still honors the original. Although the engineering took some thought, the handwork on the bag is purely intuitive—grab a color and see where it goes. I love the oddness of this piece and will have fun playing with this shape to make bags for specific purposes.
>
> The fabric-covered journal is something I often make as I work, a way to keep the ideas flowing when I'm not in the fiber studio. I gather watercolor paper between fiber covers and fill the pages with a jumbled mix of media to capture my thoughts and explore new ideas as a piece takes shape.

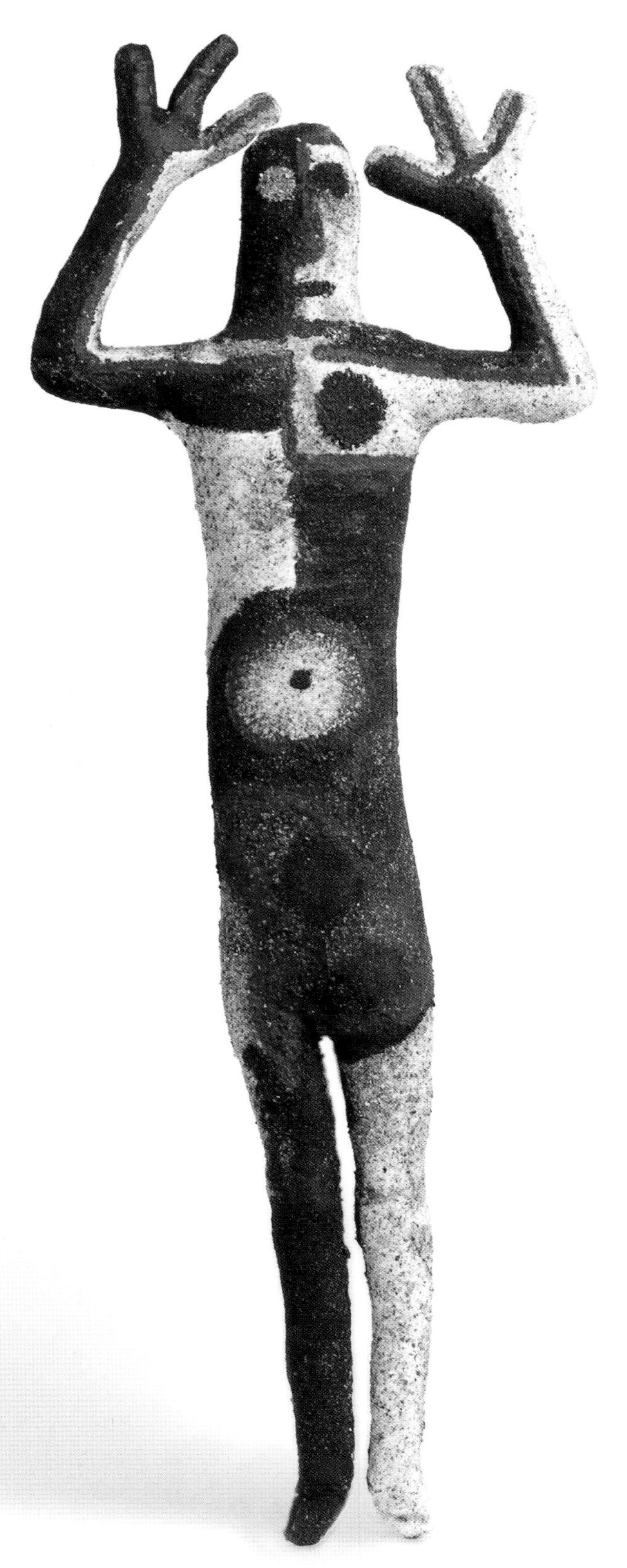

Yak Yak

Judith Harmon Hertzi

The artist writes:

> Yak Yak is an example of one of the first upright *Homo sapiens* that would be distinguished by an extraordinary achievement. He illustrated his world and possibly laughed for the first time as he did so. Surely, he was amazed that he had made a mark that, when combined with other marks, looked like his fellow human beings on the hunt for animals to sustain them. Possibly, he soon realized that he had a new power to make beautiful lines on his walls and he raised his arms in an expression of awe at what he had done.
>
> His art expressions, alight with color from the natural environment, were made approximately 30,000 years ago. Yak Yak is a spirit of the beginning of *Homo sapiens*, who until this time had been primarily concerned with making tools with which to survive.
>
> He was made very simply. I put gesso on the cloth, then added glue, and covered with sand. After this was very dry, I used dry pigment and glue and applied it with my fingers a pinch at a time. I took into account the colors that were available to him from berries, stones, and probably flowers. There was also some acrylic paint used.

Archimblad Monrovish

John Murphy

The artist writes:

> Archimblad is one of those guys who'd like to be connected with some kind of primal culture, but alas, grew up Waspy in a suburb somewhere clean. He's probably an office jockey of some high-tech start-up company, having barely any time to go home and sleep, let alone to find a social life.
>
> I varied from the pattern almost entirely, wanting to see how I personally connected with petroglyphs and primal, simplistic representation of the figure. I tried to keep Archimblad narrow and lengthy, in keeping with that simplicity. His colors were chosen from an array of upholstery samples I've got in my studio, mainly for their contrast. I gave him a haphazard "primalish" tattoo job with latex wall paint, almost as if he'd done it himself in a fit of annoyance with the organized modern world. Archimblad shrugs as if to seek acceptance by an obscured, abstract tribal history to which he may or may not be an heir. I opted to forego fingers and toes to steer clear of too much literal interpretation. Archimblad is my first "upholstryglyph."
>
> Whenever I design a stuffed toy, one measurement and one cut of the fabric leads to another measurement. Each step builds off the first. I have a very rough idea of where I want to go with a design, and ultimately I let the materials and techniques guide the finished form. Craftsmanship is always paramount, and sometimes creativity takes a backseat to making sure each seam is sound.

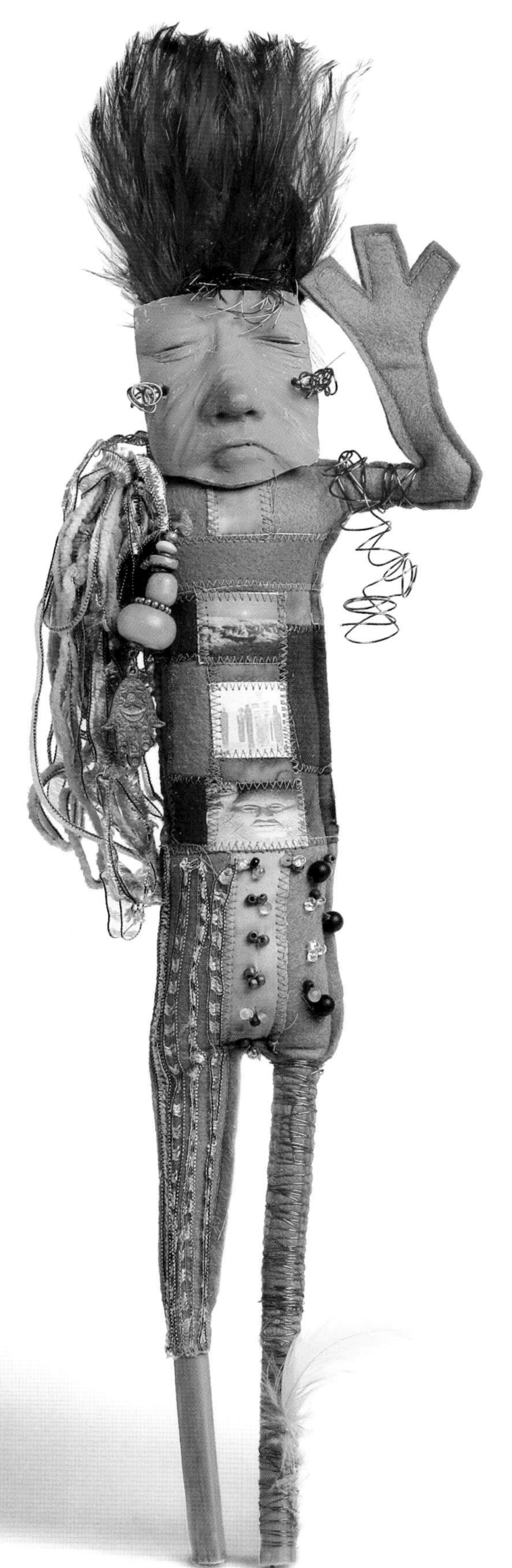

Wupatki

Rosie Rojas

The artist writes:

> I used Li's pattern as it was sent. I cut out the two body pieces. I chose one for the front and sewed the computerized images onto the front and embellished the rest with colorful yarns. I appliquéd a snakelike creature onto the back side of the body, and sewed the front to the back with a zigzag stitch, leaving an opening for the stuffing and legs to be inserted. Once it was stuffed, I sewed the side opening and glued into place the plant stems that I used as feet. I sculpted and sewed the polymer face in to place, and for extra security glued it down adding the feather headdress along with the curled copper wire that I used to disguise the threads. I also added some copper wires to the headdress.

Cowboy Slim

Rivkah Rosenfeld

The artist writes:

> This pattern inspired themes of the Wild West. It brought back childhood memories of watchin' old cowboy movies with my daddy. I decided to make my doll a "shoot-'em-down, root'n toot'n cowboy" with a sense of humor and a message about my feelings for art, the creative process, and you folks who give it a whirl.
>
> I chose the doll's heart as the focal point. Seeing as how my theme is about freedom of artistic creativity, I cut the heart right outta there to suggest the idea of runnin' free in the wild blue yonder.
>
> The hat and boots were created with polymer clay. The hat was painted black, covered in glue, and sprinkled with mohair snips for a wool felt effect. The boots are imprinted with a floral-motif rubber stamp. The face is a mask created with polymer clay. Is that a wink or did he lose an eye in a shoot-out? I think he's winking, because he knows we all like his hat! The caption tags on the hat, heart, and ATC were created by printing on to watercolor paper after the paper was treated with "distress ink" and then torn out.
>
> The pistol is a vintage copyright-free image transferred to fabric, then sewn and stuffed.
>
> The cigarette is built on a piece of wire. The wire is wrapped with floral tape and a tiny bit of stuffing, then "rolled" with cigarette paper cut to fit. A tiny bit of tobacco is glued on the very tip. The wire protrudes a scant 1/16" (1.6 mm) at the "butt" so that it can be inserted in to the doll's mouth.

Now, this doll was an open palette for artistic imagination. He had me blazin' the trails the whole way through the creative process! I hope my cowboy opens your creative heart as he did mine. And remember, "A cowboy's heart weighs as much as a buffalo, and is as full as a barrel of moonshine!"

> "I take no sass but sarsaparilla."
>
> —John Wesley Hardin

Goddess iconography has been my passion for years, as evidenced by my very first patterns of the Boulder Goddess. She is a morphing of the Venus of Willendorf, the Bird Goddess, and an Akuaba fertility figure. The shapes fit so well together! They are so perfectly Girlie, delighting the playful in us, while at the same time so beautifully, viscerally Woman, striking the sonorous chord of authentic femininity.

Chapter 5: Creativity

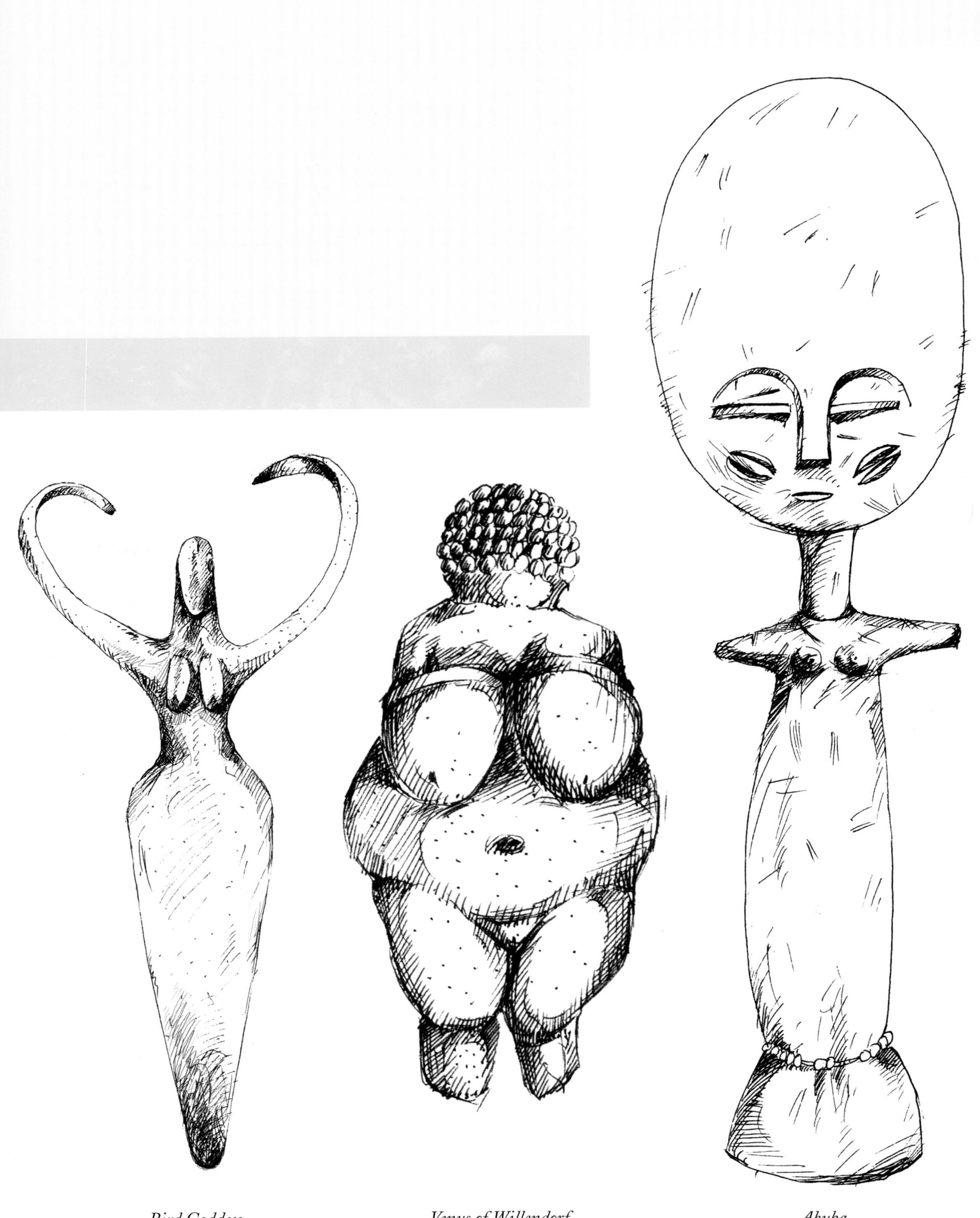

Bird Goddess *Venus of Willendorf* *Akuba*

Our Lady of Eureka: Embracing the New

THE DUAL PERSONALITY DOLL OF THIS CHAPTER came from a study of the Christian saint, Our Lady of Guadalupe and the Paleolithic Bird Goddess. Our Lady ripples and dances in luminescence, her story rich with the essence of compassion, while her bird goddess influences represent the realm of creation and regeneration. Her upraised arms, like the perfect circle of the seasons, bring life to Earth.

Our Lady of Guadalupe.

Our Lady of Guadalupe has a wonderful story. On December 12, 1531, Juan Diego was passing the hill of Tepeyac on his way to pray when he heard music so beautiful that he thought he might be in heaven. He looked toward the top of the hill and there was a beautiful young, pregnant, woman calling his name. She seemed to be dressed in the sun, and the stars were in her cape. He knew by the brooch she wore that she was the mother of Jesus. She asked him where he was going and he told her that he was on his way to Tlatelolco to listen to the Mexican friars there. She smiled and said that she was "the eternally consummate Virgin, Saint Mary, mother of the very true deity, God, the giver of life, the creator of people, the ever present, the Lord of Heaven and Earth." Juan must have been a bit stunned! When she asked him to go to the bishop and tell him that she wanted a temple built on the very spot they were standing so she could attend to the healing of the sorrows and afflictions of those who loved her, Juan questioned his ability to convince the bishop that this was actually happening. She then produced Castilian roses, which are not usually found in the deserts of Mexico in December, and instructed him to gather them up in his tilma, a cloak made of cactus fiber. Off he went with his cloak of blooms and when he and the bishop opened the cloak, there was a beautiful image of the Virgin miraculously burned into the fabric! (Some say the very cape that Juan Diego wore is in the Basilica of Guadalupe in Mexico City). Needless to say, the bishop built a spectacular church.

One can look at the image on the cape and the subsequent ubiquitous Guadalupes on everything from votive candles to tea cozies and find what historians claim is a pictograph that the ancient Aztecs would have easily understood. She stands in front of the sun, obscuring the wrathful sun god: Huitzilopochtli. She stands on top of the moon, crushing the symbol embraced by the god Quetzalcoatl. Just her stance effectively wipes out these most bloodthirsty of Aztec gods. The stars on her mantle reflect the constellations as they were on the day she appeared to Juan, and the royal blue-green color shows she is queen. The black Aztec maternity belt proves she is pregnant. And finally, the pattern of her rose-colored dress is a contour map of Mexico. She is so full of symbolism and story!

Our Lady brought peace and healing to these oppressed people. In our world today, she is emblematic of strength, compassion, regeneration, and love. In our doll, she is represented by her pregnant belly, her sweet and loving face, and the secret strength in her upraised arms.

The Bird Goddess and Our Lady are both referred to as "life givers." The Bird Goddess was traditionally called upon to "bring forth," for example, you might put a little goddess figure in the grain bin to bring a wealth of crops, in the kitchen to bring food, or in the bed to bring ba-

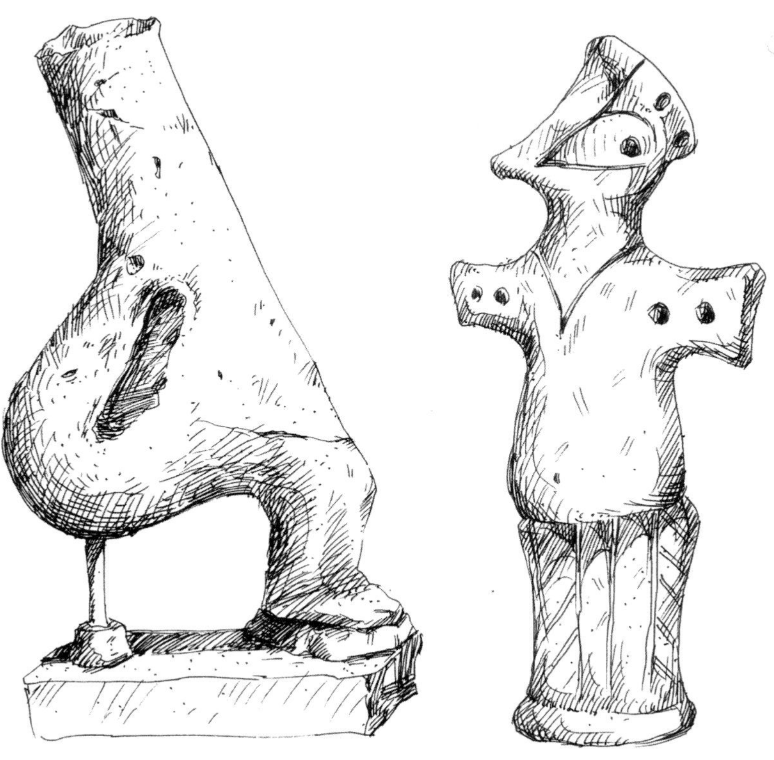

Big Behind bird goddess

Lady Bird

bies. She was seen as the Cosmic Creator, the bringer of life force from the sun to the Earth. With her upraised, welcoming arms you can't help but feel her strength.

The hunter-gatherers of ancient times saw the water bird's migration as emblematic of the seasons of the year as well as the seasons of life. Spring will come, you will die, and others will be born; life moves on. From this idea, they created hybrid women water birds, with long necks, often with big behinds with an egg or fish hidden inside, sometimes with wings, beaks, and chevrons as decoration.

Marija Gimbutas, author of the groundbreaking book *Civilization of the Goddess*, believes the parallel lines, chevrons, and rhythmic meandering patterns found on ancient artifacts from ritual objects to the walls of caves and shrines represent the Bird Goddess and her sister, the Snake Goddess.

The goddess below is a perfect example of this with her wing-stump arms, her many lines, and her stance, ready to leap in to the air!

She also comments that the Bird Goddess may be associated with the creation of the music of the spheres. This theory comes from the evidence of so many ancient flutes and drums covered in bird goddess art.

Our doll is full of joyful music. She dances wildly yet she can also be composed and gentle; anchored to the fertile earth. This goddess embodies the full essence of "woman," so how could we have just one pattern?!

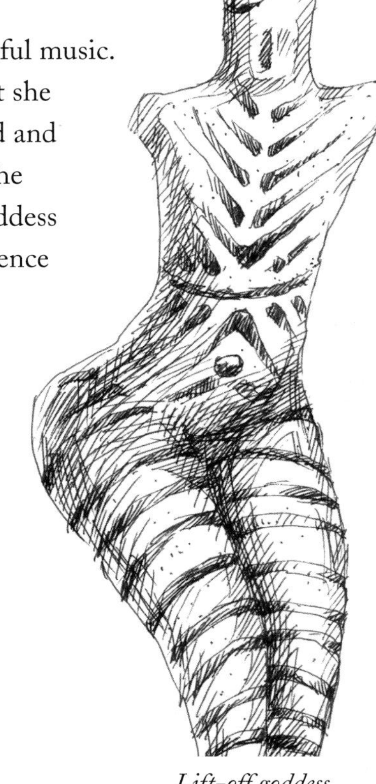

Lift-off goddess

Musings

Why not play with these motifs? In your doll book (page 18), open to a page that seems right and begin drawing chevrons nested in to each other. Draw parallel lines. Draw zigzags for water, draw Xs and fill them with chevrons. Try adding some of your favorite symbols to the mix. Do not be afraid to draw on top of earlier drawings, as I did, or color outside the lines—in fact, please, color outside the lines!

Materials

- basics, embellishing, painting and drawing, and sculpting kits (page 12)
- fat quarter of tight-weave cotton fabric for each body
- two pieces of 8" × 12" (20.3 × 30.5 cm) cotton fabric for the back of the wings and the collage base
- 8" (20.3 cm) square of tulle for the wing collage
- collage embellishments for the arms and wings (Note: You must be able to sew through all of the wing collage materials.)
- 8" (20.3 cm) square of dense, low-loft cotton batting such as Warm and Natural Cotton Batting for the wings
- yarn or other material for the hair (page 101)
- matching sewing thread
- embroidery thread for the embroidered face (optional)
- 1" (2.5 cm) button for removable wings (optional)
- beeswax for reinforcing the thread
- pipe cleaners for embellishing the wrists and shoulders (optional)
- 19" (48.3 cm) of 20- or 14-gauge galvanized steel wire for the arms

- 12½" (31.8 cm) of wire, the same gauge as the arms (or finer) for the fingers
- 42" (106.7 cm) of 18-gauge wire for the skirt: steel, copper or found (Note: If you are using found wire, be very careful about rust around your delicate, ever-so-pokeable skin!)
- 25" (63.5 cm) of 22-gauge (or finer) beading wire for the skirt
- small bead (⅛" [3 mm] circumference) for the nose
- beads with holes large enough to slide on to the wire for the skirt
- low-tack, quick-release masking tape for the arms

Tools

- air- or water-soluble ink to mark the buttonhole on the wings (optional)
- sharp tapestry or yarn needle for poking large holes
- stamps for the paper clay arms
- wire cutters

Adventurer's Materials and Tools

- two 10" (25.4 cm) squares of tight-weave cotton for the body, gusset, wings, and tail (Note: One square can be a contrasting fabric.)
- 2½" (6.4 cm) squares of felt: one matching the body fabric and one white and one black for the eyes
- 10" (25.4 cm) square of dense cotton batting such as Warm and Natural Cotton Batting for the wings and tail
- embroidery thread in matching and contrasting colors
- one small black bead for the eye
- 22" (55.9 cm) length of 18-gauge wire: steel, copper or "found" for the legs
- Pipe-Cleaner Plumage (page 71)
- thumbnail-size piece of paper clay such as Creative Paperclay or Delight Modeling Compound for the beak

Body

This pattern has two heads and two bodies, a veritable plethora of possibilities. The Our Lady of Eureka body dances and is a little harder to make. The Most High Sun Bird Goddess body is the traditional bird goddess form.

Have fun playing with the different options, or choose one and create her as explained in this chapter.

Our Lady of Eureka

This body is unique in that the legs are meant to cross, as if she is making an enthusiastic jump skyward.

1. Trace the body pattern pieces (page 120-123) on to cardboard and cut them out. Use a bent leg front and a bent leg back on one half of the body and a straight leg back to a straight leg front on the other side. Also, you can choose from a slight (skinny minny) belly and a fuller one (great goddess belly). Be sure to use the same belly for both fronts of your doll.
2. Trace around each pattern piece on the wrong side of a single layer of a fat quarter.
3. Cut out, adding a ¼" (6 mm) seam allowance. A wider seam allowance makes it easier to match up the different legs.
4. Sew down the back, leaving a gap where indicated.
5. Sew the fronts together.
6. Lay the body pieces right sides together. Match the shoulders, waist, and legs and carefully pin in place (a).
7. Sew around the entire doll.
8. Turn and stuff firmly. Sew up the hole, leaving a ⅛" (3 mm) hole at the top, which is where you attach the wire and lace skirt.

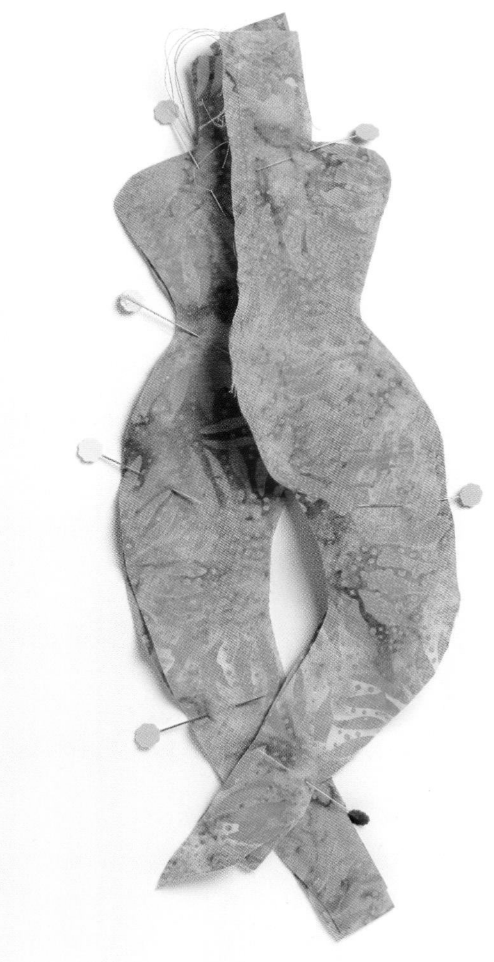

(a)
Pinned and ready to sew.

Musings

It is only in the last half century or so that the term washboard has been associated with bellies rather than hard labor. Throughout the centuries, goddess figures have been voluptuous, and when I say that I don't mean just a little pudgy, I mean built like a substantial woman! Consider paying particular attention to the belly of your Lady; what you might add here speaks of the weight of fertility, grace of curve, and essence of the vessel of life.

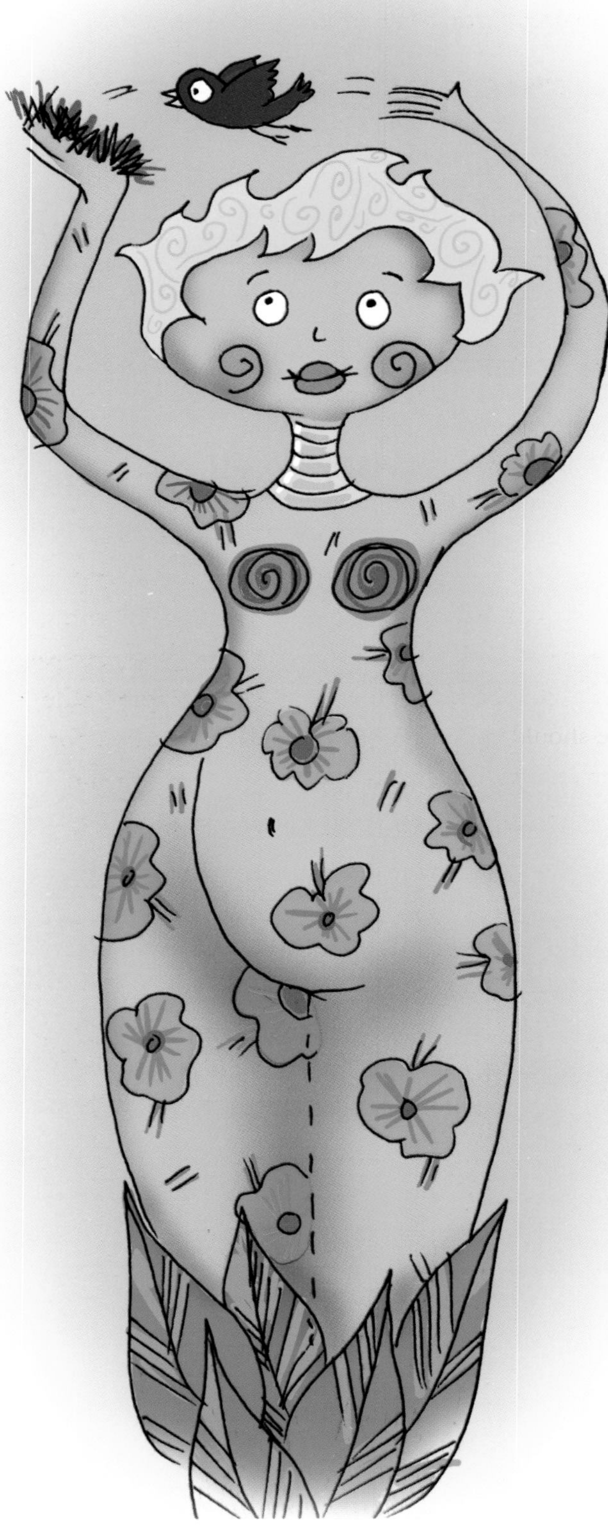

The Most High Sun Bird Goddess

This body has legs that at first look like they are trapped in a gunny sack waiting for the race to begin, but once you sculpt them, they look quite shapely.

1. Trace the pattern pieces (pages 124-125) on to cardboard and cut them out. There is only one leg extension pattern piece in the pattern. Trace and cut two shapes; tape one to the body front and one to the body back.

Tip

Here is where you can extend even more! You can make a very tall goddess by making the body longer before you tape it to the leg extension.

2. Fold the fat quarter right sides together and trace both the front and back onto the fabric.
3. Sew the layers together from the neck to the toes on the nonshoulder sides (center back and center front), leaving a gap where indicated.
4. Cut out the stitched shapes.
5. Splay front on back, pinning if necessary.
6. Sew around the entire doll, leaving the neck top open.
7. Turn the doll right side out and stuff the neck, shoulders, and belly firmly. Stuff the legs less firmly. Sew up the gap on the body, leaving an 1/8" (3 mm) opening at the bottom for attaching the skirt.
8. With a doll sculpting needle and waxed thread, start at the X and go through from the back, make a strong knot, and return the needle through the body to the front (b). Continue stitching all the way down to the bottom of the legs.

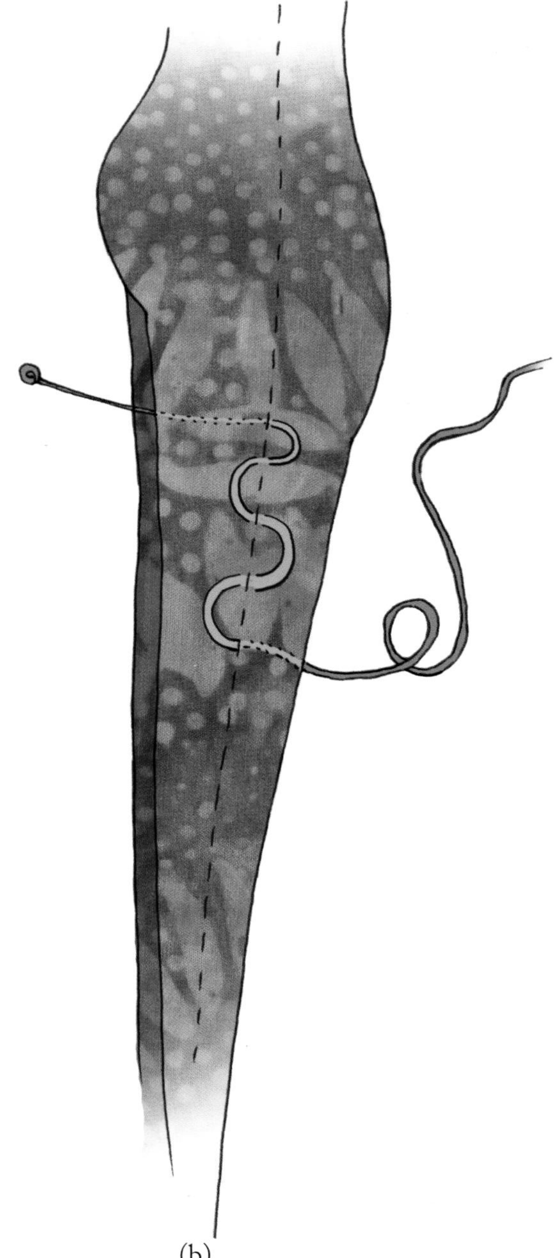

(b)
Pull the thread taut as you sew each leg.

9. With a running stitch, hand sew all of the way to the bottom of the doll, finishing with a stitch that comes out on the back. Tie a strong knot, and hide the thread in the doll.

10. Massage the legs to make them more three-dimensional.

Arms

These are unique, multimaterial appendages

1. Straighten the first 6" (15.2 cm) of the arm wire.

2. With the big sharp tapestry needle, poke a hole in one shoulder and insert the wire.

Tip

Cut the wire on an angle to make it slightly pointy and easier to insert.

3. With a back-and-forth twisting motion to keep the stuffing from bunching, gently push the wire through the width of the body to emerge at the opposite shoulder. When you can feel the wire inside the shoulder, use a large needle to make a hole for it to emerge. Push more of the wire through and center it on the body (c).

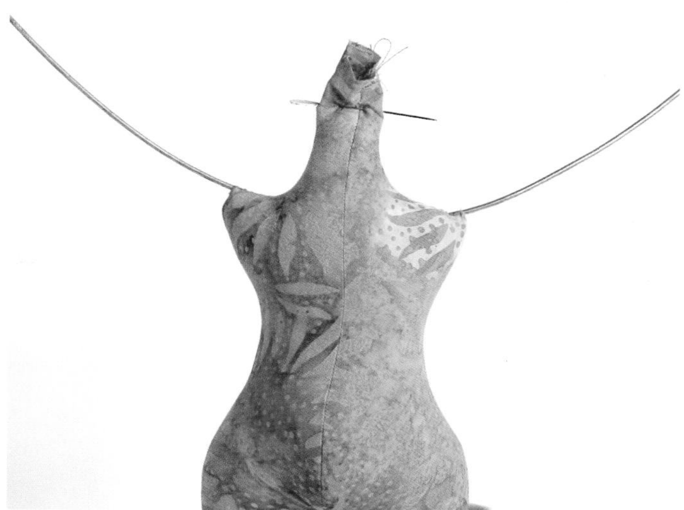

(c)
Use a single strand of wire for both arms.

4. Make masking tape clay guards by taping on the body around where the wire comes out (d). Paper clay residue can be hard to remove, so use lots of tape.

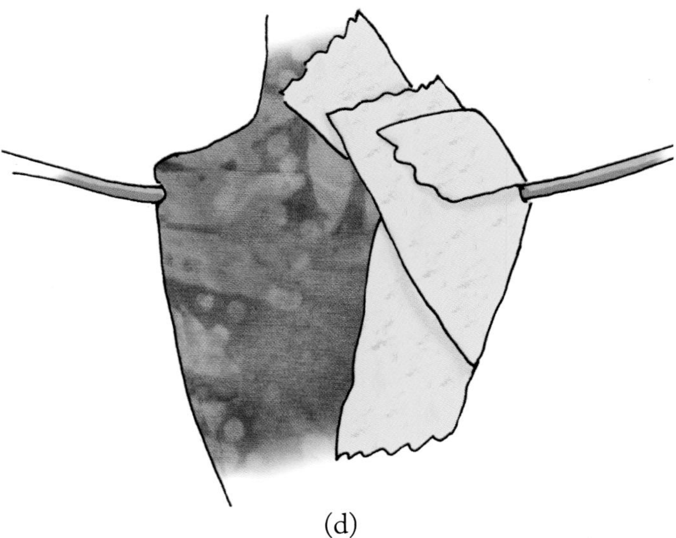

(d)
Protect the fabric with masking tape guards.

5. In general, an arm is a little longer from the shoulder to the elbow than it is from the elbow to the wrist. Measure the wire from the shoulder down 2¼" (5.7 cm) and make the elbow bend. There will be long forearms of extra wire. If you want raised arms, bend them up. End the wrist at just before 3" (7.6 cm).

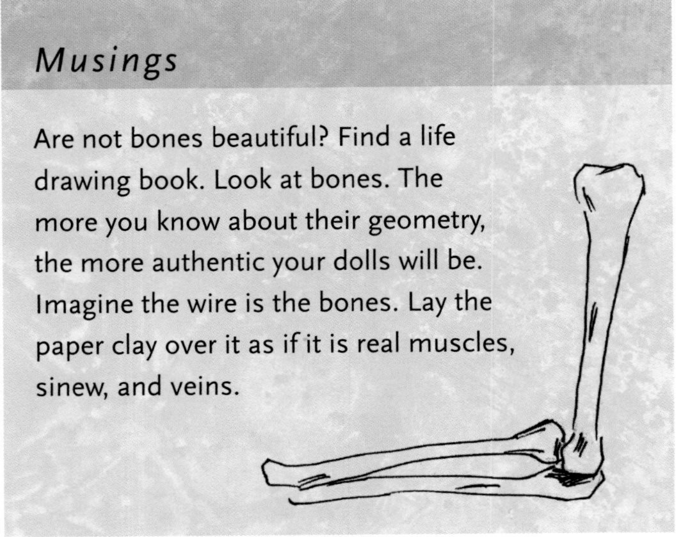

Musings

Are not bones beautiful? Find a life drawing book. Look at bones. The more you know about their geometry, the more authentic your dolls will be. Imagine the wire is the bones. Lay the paper clay over it as if it is real muscles, sinew, and veins.

6. Do not cut off the excess wire yet. Roll the paper clay into a ½" (1.3 cm) -wide worm and work it around the wire. Smooth any rough places with water. Try using stamps or other objects to impress patterns in to the paper clay while it is damp (e).

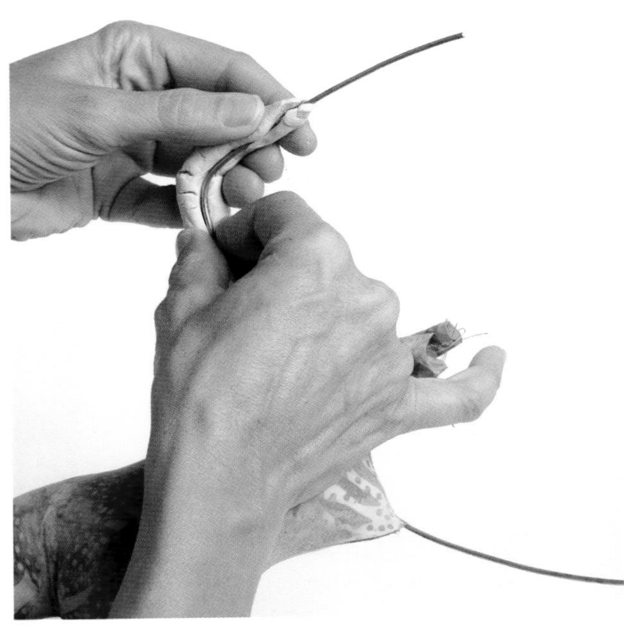

(e)
Mold clay around the wire.

7. Let the paper clay dry completely, sand any rough edges, then apply a coat of gesso.

8. Paint the arms and embellish or collage (page 102) and then apply polyurethane.

Hands

1. Snip ten 1¼" (3.2 cm) -long pieces of wire and make a small hoop at the top of each one.

2. Roll ten little paper clay balls (or sausage shapes) for the tips of the fingers. Put the hoop part of the wire in to the balls and smoosh the entry point to ensure that the finger tips never fall off.

3. Make a soft-edged square for the palm. Poke a hole straight into the middle of the palm, for the thumb wire. Poke four holes in the top (f). Push the wrist side of the palm onto the arm wire. Let dry.

(f)
Use the thumb wire to make a decorative palm.

4. After they are bone-dry, apply gesso to all of the pieces.

5. Paint the shapes, add glitter, perhaps collage (page 102). Cover with polyurethane.

6. Trim the wire to the length you want. Glue each finger in to the palm.

7. Trim the thumb wire to twice as long as the finished length. Make a ⅛" (3 mm) -long, 45-degree angle at the end. Poke the bent part into the hand. Bend the exposed wire around to create a curlicue on the palm. Glue the wire in to the palm.

8. Snip the wire at the wrist edge of the arm ¼" (6 mm) from the fleshy part of the arm (g).

(g)
Let exposed wire act as the wrist.

Tip

Painting wire is easy if you first swipe it with a little paint thinner or gesso. Some paints can be applied directly to wire.

9. Paint the wire to match the arm.
10. Glue the hand on, wrap an embellished pipe cleaner, beads, or yarn around the wrist and at the shoulders to hide the wire.

Head

These instructions are set up so that Our Lady of Eureka has the Gentle Head, which is wider, and the Sun Bird Goddess has the Impish Head (below). The Sun Bird Goddess head is a little more pear-shaped, with big poofy cheeks—no doubt full of nuts or something outstandingly healthy.

1. Trace the desired front and back head pattern pieces (page 122) onto cardboard and cut them out.
2. With right sides of two fabric pieces together, trace around the desired head front. Trace around the Impish Head Back if you are making the Sun Bird Goddess. For Our Lady of Eureka, trace the Gentle Head Back on the wrong side of a single layer of fabric.

3. Sew the nose side of the head front through both layers. For the Sun Bird Goddess, sew the Impish Head backs together along the less curved edge, for the center back. Cut out, adding a seam allowance wherever there is a seam.

4. Open the seamed pieces and, with right sides together, put the front on the back. Sew around the whole head. For Our Lady of Eureka (gentle) head cut a small hole on the back, toward the top of the head, where the hair will cover it; leave a gap in the Sun Bird Goddess' head seam, as marked on the Impish Head back pattern piece.

5. Turn the head right side out.

6. Sew a nose bead in the tip of the nose (see the tip box on page 30). Stuff the nose firmly.

7. Embroider the face or, if you plan to paint it, continue with the following section.

Painting a Pretty Face for Our Lady

Your imagination is the only limit for this face. For guidance, look at the diagram (h).

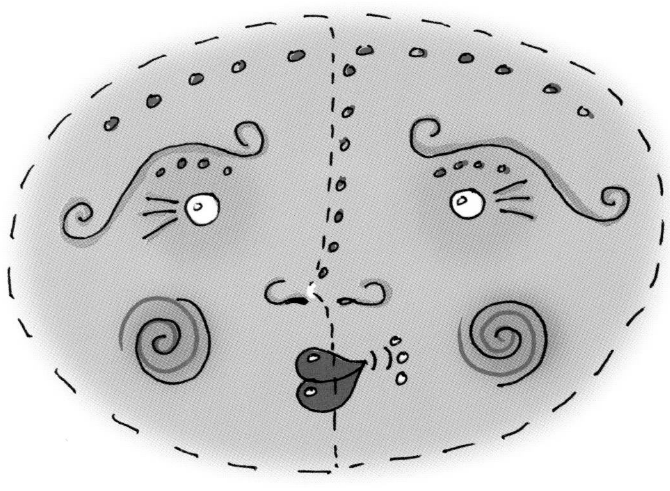

(h)
Follow this illustration when adding face details.

1. Apply gesso to the face area. Let dry. Paint the base of the face the color of the fabric, or a wild contrasting color!

2. This doll has a very wide head, so think about where you want the eyes. Should they be big and close together, giving her that just-saw-a-giant-hairy-spider-sticking-out-of-the-bun look, or small and far apart with the open-sky-happy-day look that says "Y'all want the sweetened iced tea, of course"? Make a light pencil mark on the face where you want each eye.

(i)
Explore a rainbow of eyebrow expressions.

Musings

It might be fun to paint some of the motifs from your fabric or maybe something you would like to evoke on the face, as I did with the yellow leaves that mirror the foliage dancing up her leg.

3. Do you want her to have a surprised look? Nudge up the eyebrows, so they are higher on the forehead. Perhaps she is a little miffed because the Blue Chickie of Happiness (page 104) is scratching around in the tomatoes? For this look, bring the eyebrows down near the bridge of the nose and up toward the ears (i).

4. Paint a gentle swirl under the nose and add a curlicue to each cheek.

5. This simple lip was designed with Picasso in mind. It is a side view on a front-view face. Paint two little raindrops that are turned on their side and pinched together at one end.

Attaching the Head

1. Turn the top, raw edges of the neck to the inside. Stuff firmly to the top.

2. Firmly stitch the head on the neck.

3. Use beads, wire, and other decorative elements to enhance the neck.

Hair

When you apply hair, always consider alternative materials. Of course, yarn is an obvious and wonderful choice, but what about beads, carpeting, curly pasta noodles, fabric, fake flowers, feathers, felt, fur, found objects, nails, paint, paper, steel wool, straw, a swimming cap, thread, toys, wire, or wood? The list is, obviously, endless.

Sew the hair down by hand. Use matching thread and big stitches in a general swirl pattern, from the very top of the head to the back of the neck.

Making Curly Hair

The very best way to make wild curly hair is to use an electric drill.

1. Find a screw eye big enough to thread your yarn through and put it in to the drill where the bits usually go. Tighten carefully.

Creativity Exercise:

Consider a Neck Extension

It is all the rage to do lovely dolls with very long, elegant necks. Here is a handy neck extension technique that is specially suited for anyone who might find herself swathed in jewels, like, say, a goddess.

1. With card stock, make a cone the height of the desired extension (to a maximum of 4½" [11.4 cm]), and a little wider than the neck. Tape the edges to temporarily hold the shape.

2. Cut out half-moon shapes where the wider bottom edge meets the shoulders, so the cone sits nicely on the doll.

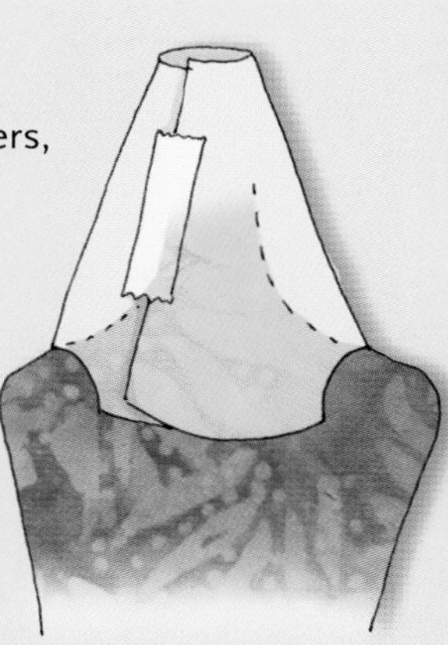

3. Wrap pipe cleaners with delectable fabric morsels and augment with beads, yarn, and other goodies.

4. Wrap the pipe cleaners around the cone. Sew them together.

5. Remove the card stock cone. Place the pipe cleaner cone on the neck. Sew or glue firmly.

6. Sew the head to the neck extension.

7. Place the bottom of the cone on the shoulders and sew the base to the doll. The doll's neck will be hidden by the extension.

2. Cut yarn strands to 15 feet (4.6 m) -long. (Note: Eyelash and furry yarn will be delightfully spikey.) The finished hair will be one-third the length of the yarn that you start with. Gather the yarn strands together, twirl them by hand into a single length, and thread this into the screw eye and tie.

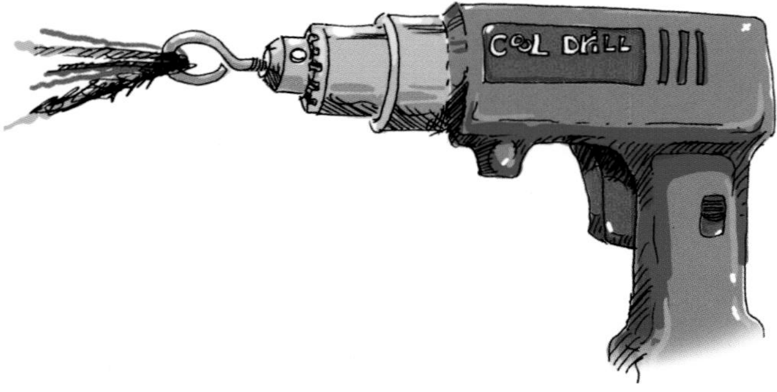

3. Tie the opposite end of the yarn length to a doorknob, or get someone to hold it for you.

4. Pull the yarn taut, hold the drill firmly and turn it on. The yarn will wind around itself. When you let up on the pressure a bit, the yarn turns into wonderful curls.

5. You can add fabric, more yarn, or paper by dropping the new item in to the moving yarn.

6. Cut the yarn off the doorknob and the screw eye.

I learned this wonderful technique from Barbara Chapman in a class where she was making the most amazing necklaces, so consider making several strands just in case you need some raw material for another project!

Wings

What better method of transportation for a bird goddess, eh? And collage is such a nice way to indulge in your urge to embellish! The wings are created by making collage fabric and then cutting the pattern shapes from it.

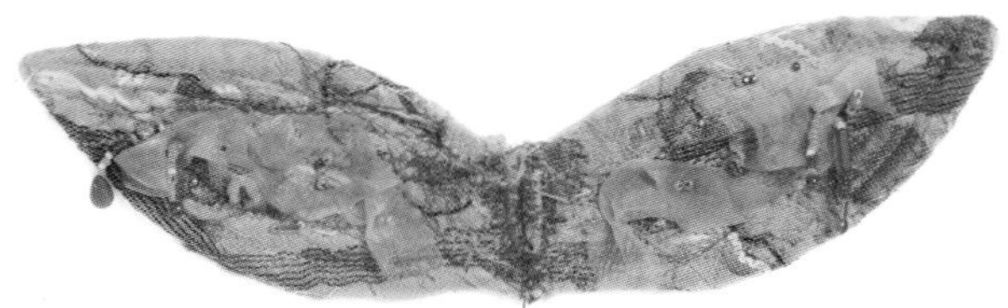

1. Lay the collage base fabric, right side up, on a table.

2. Arrange your collage embellishments, right side up, on top of the base fabric.

3. Place tulle over the collage and pin the layers together all over the surface (j).

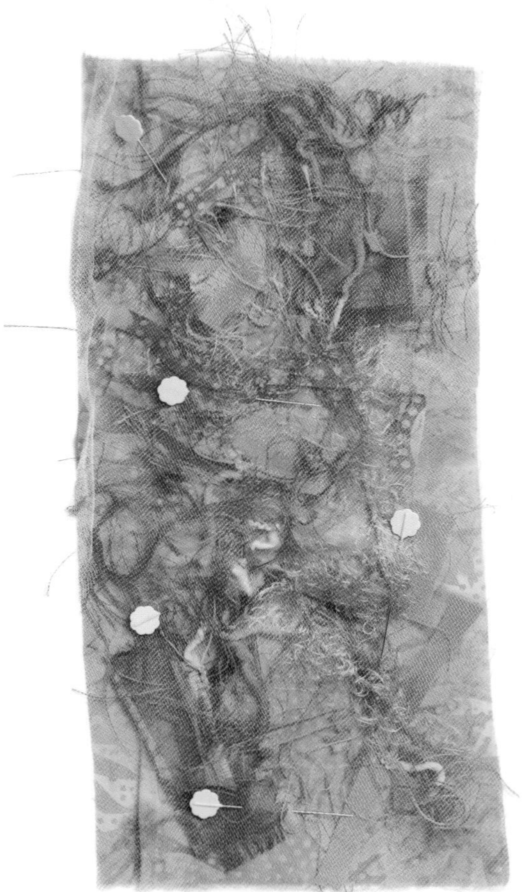

(j)
Hold everything in place with pins.

4. Sew just enough to hold everything in place, using a long machine stitch.

Musings

When making a collage, I sew meandering lines and then play with the decorative stitches, change the thread color, go back and forth with gusto in one spot to create density, loop around and, finally, reluctantly, stop somewhere on the outer edge.

5. Place a layer of cotton batting underneath the wrong side of the collage, then place another piece of cotton fabric for the back of the wings on top, with the right side facing the collage (k).

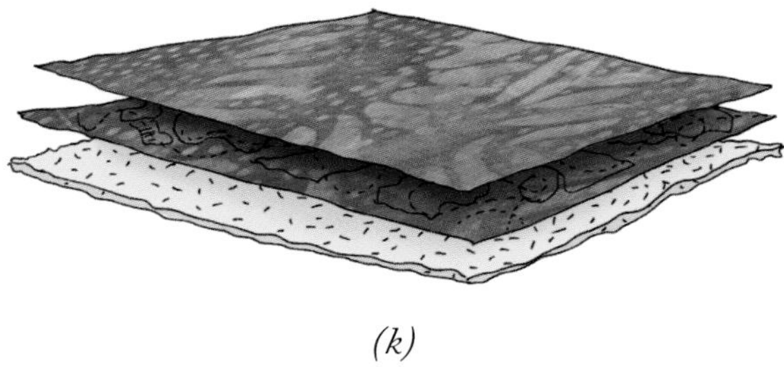

(k)

Stack batting on the bottom, collage in the center, and the wing back on top.

6. Trace a wing on top. Flip the wing pattern piece upside down and trace another wing on the fabric stack. Use a pen with air- or water-soluble ink to mark the optional buttonhole position on both wings.
7. Sew around, leaving the flat part open on each wing.
8. Turn and topstitch (quilt) a feathery pattern into the wings.
9. Sew the wings to the doll. Or, for removable wings, butt together the flat parts. Sew the top and bottom of the butted edges together with zigzag stitches, leaving open where indicated, to make a buttonhole.
10. Attach a button to the doll and button the wings on. Voila! Removable wings!

Wire Skirt

After your doll is finished, you can make her a beaded wire skirt.

1. With 18-gauge wire, make a 45-degree bend ¼" (6 mm) from an end.
2. Stick the bent part into your doll where you left the small hole after stuffing.
3. Shape the wire into a spiral around the doll, with the bottom being the widest. Think of hoop skirts.
4. String beads along the wire.
5. With lighter wire, cut pieces that will span the levels, bead them, and then wrap the wire several times horizontally around the thicker wire tiers (l).

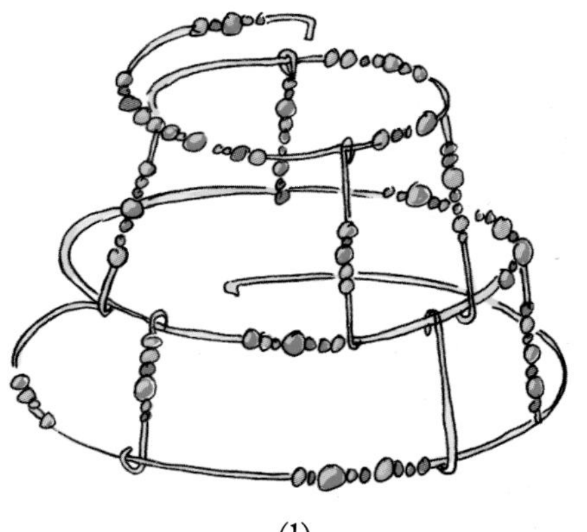

(l)

Secure the spiral with horizontal wires.

6. Tie or stitch diaphanous (light, delicate, almost transparent) fabric scraps to the wires (m).

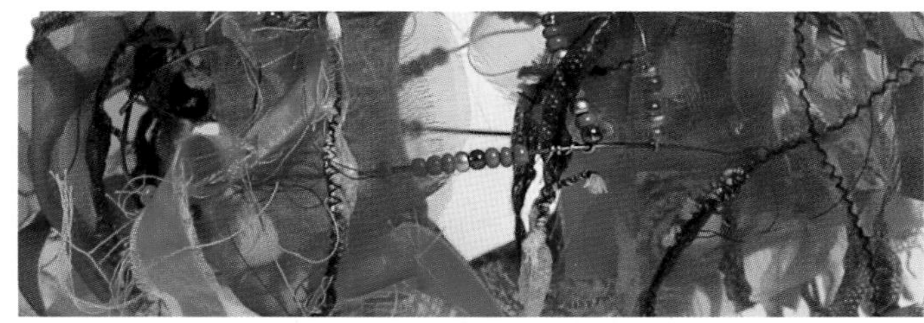

(m)

Tie on scraps to give the skirt more volume.

7. Glue the skirt in place or just leave it anchored in the hole so it can come on and off.

Creativity Exercise:

Adventurer's Project: Blue Chickie of Happiness

All goddesses need sidekicks and this is the perfect one for your goddess. In addition, it is a well-known, even documented, bringer of a hearty grin. She has no Paleolithic precursor, no dark mysterious caves for her. She is the symbol of all that is love and happiness and hope. She is the perfect companion for a goddess.

Preparing the Pattern

1. Gather the Adventurer's Materials and Tools (page 91).
2. Trace the pattern pieces (page 124) on cardboard and cut them out.

Wings

1. Lay the fabric squares, right sides together, on top of a single layer of cotton batting.
2. Trace two wing shapes. Sew around the wings, leaving open where noted.
3. Cut out the shapes and turn them right side out.
4. Topstitch as indicated on the pattern piece.

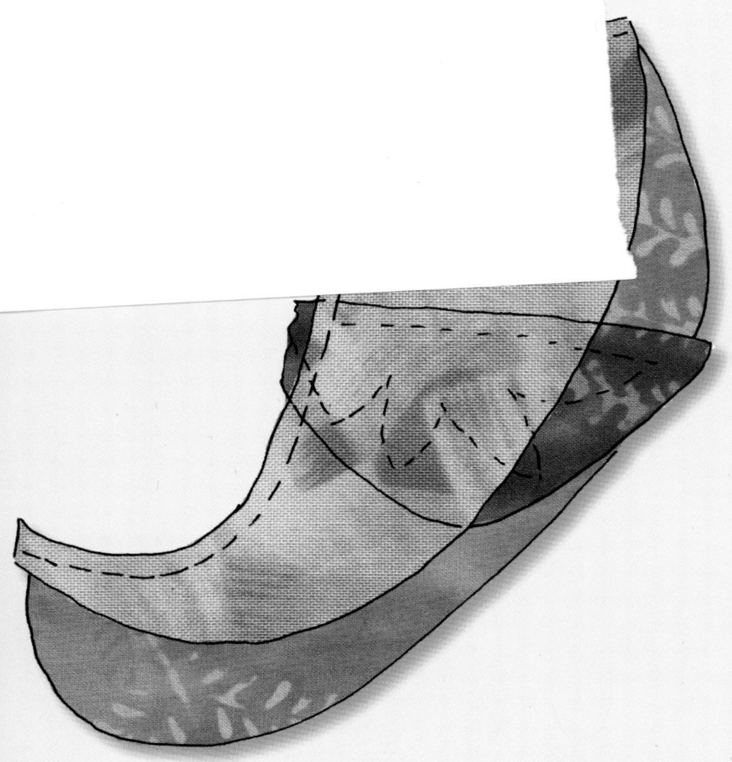

5. Attach the opposite side of the gusset to the remaining wing and body piece in the same manner.
6. With right sides together, sew together the remaining edges of the body pieces.
7. Cut a hole where an eye is indicated, and turn the body right side out.
8. Stuff firmly. Sew up the hole.

Body

1. With the right sides of the fabric together, trace around the body, and cut out the shapes.
2. Cut one gusset from a single layer of fabric.
3. Place one body piece, right side up, on a table. Lay one wing on top, where indicated, with the raw edges even. Place the gusset, wrong side up, on top, matching the triangles.
4. Sew along one side of the gusset, through all layers, from top to bottom.

Tail

1. Lay two fabric pieces right sides together (make one piece a contrasting color). Place a piece of cotton batting on top. Trace a tail shape. Sew around the shapes, leaving open where noted. Cut out the shape and turn it right side out.
2. Tuck the extra fabric into the tail, hiding the cotton batting. Topstitch across the end to close it.
3. Topstitch as indicated on the pattern piece.
4. Sew the tail to the bird's behind.

Eyes

1. Cut out each part of the eye from the felt.
2. Working on one eye at a time, stack the eye pieces. Hand sew the layers together and sew a bead (the pupil) so that the bird looks in the direction you choose. Make the second eye in the same way.
3. Use a blanket stitch to sew the lower layer of each eye to the bird, being sure to cover the turning hole on one side of the head.
4. Attach Pipe-Cleaner Plumage (page 71) to the bird's head.

Beak

1. Roll a small, beak-sized cone of paper clay. Insert wire in the wide end, as you did for the goddess finger balls (page 97). Let dry
2. Paint the beak with gesso. Let dry.
3. Paint with acrylic.
4. When dry, poke the beak in to the front seam of the bird and then glue it to the head.

Legs

1. Cut an 11" (27.9 cm) piece of wire. Bend the wire in half. Hold the bent area and twist the wires until the twisted area is 1/2" (1.3 cm) long. This makes a toe.
2. Twist the doubled wire on each side of the first toe, to create two more toes.
3. Twist the wire to create a 2 1/2" (6.4 cm) -long leg. Make a second leg in the same way.
4. Create two holes with a large needle on the bottom of the bird, one for each leg. Insert the top of each leg in a hole and hot glue it in place.
5. Use scrap fabric and yarn to decorate the tail, the top of the legs, and the wings.
6. Introduce your bird to your goddess.

I wish you all the richly creative lives, full of bluebirds flittering around you so thickly that you can hardly see the beautiful blue sky!

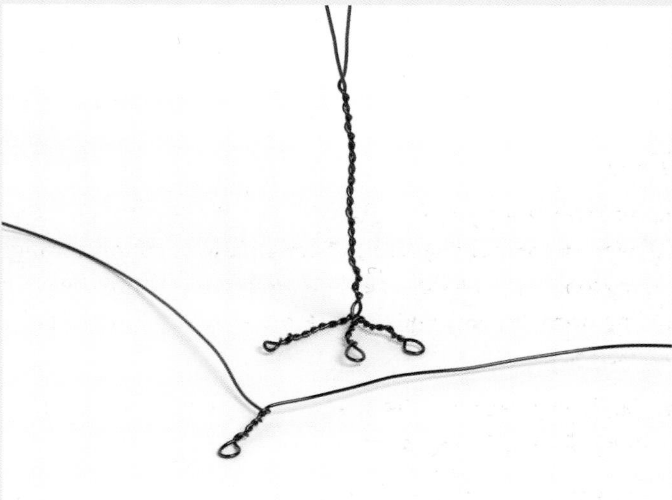

Goddess of Cherry Blossoms

Leslie Molin

The artist writes:

> Making a Goddess doll … hmmm ... how fun! My style of dollmaking lends itself to simple, clean lines with the use of Japanese and Asian fabrics. This project was a great challenge for me.
>
> To incorporate both the Goddess and Japanese themes, I thought of cherry blossoms—so delicate and beautiful. The doll would be a great Goddess of Cherry Blossoms, symbolic of spring and renewed growth.
>
> I typically design my own patterns so to use someone else's pattern was intriguing. I looked over the patterns and chose the "Other" body. The fabrics I selected were all Japanese cottons. I wanted the pattern or design on the fabric to speak for itself, so I did alter the pattern a bit.
>
> I divided the body in half by piecing two fabrics down the center. I kept the legs together and let the pieced fabric define the leg separation. The Head was kept basically the same, though I changed the facial features and added an appliqué of a flower blossom to her cheek.
>
> I could not forget the all-important obi with a lovely tie on the back; this was done with another Japanese cotton.
>
> I changed her arms and hands to kimono sleeves and added a fan of Japanese washi paper with pretty dangling ribbons. Her hair is horsehair in tribute to the Asian expertise in horse riding.
>
> All in all, this was a fun project, and I enjoyed being asked to participate in the joys and creation of a Goddess!

Gallery

Zenda

Jan Hayman

The artist writes:

> Zenda, which means womanly, is the goddess that brings life in all forms. She was created using a muslin base, painted with Lumiere paints in several colors gradating up from pinks to blues to gold. She was also stamped with gold paint in several places on her body.
>
> Her skirt was made of yarns and threads wrapped around a card as if making fringe. It was then sewn on and a hand-beaded fringe was added.
>
> Her belly and bosoms were adorned with hot-fix crystals. She has a beaded gold choker and bracelets. The area between her shoulder and upper arm is several different yarns wrapped and twisted around her connecting in the back at the base of her spine. They were tacked down with a few beads. She has a scepter made out of paper clay and painted with Lumiere paints. Her headpiece is hand-dyed emu feathers. Her face was also painted with Lumiere.

Peace Child

Linda Hansen

The artist writes:

> When I originally started this doll, my idea was for her to be leaping with joy, so I used a vibrant batik with several different colors thereby not limiting my embellishment choices. After I made the body, I added the baby dolls painted in black. I was not sure where this doll was going but liked the contrast so I continued.
>
> I cut the backs off of vintage black earrings and added those to the chest. I kept visualizing a doll with its arms outstretched with a child in its hands. It was then that I realized what I was making.
>
> I have been listening to a lot of the Iraq war stories, told from a mother's perspective, on National Public Radio. I listen not with the ears of one who hears which side is right or wrong, but as someone who mourns over the loss of children; children who are full-grown adults to children who are innocent casualties. The ones who die (or are horribly scarred) have mothers who mourn for them. This doll was my way of dealing and mourning with them. I remembered a book I had read a long time ago about a tribe that would give a child to their enemies, and in return they would receive a child back. This child was referred to as a "peace child." The child in this doll's arms is my peace child.
>
> I then made the head of the doll. I gessoed the fabric and painted it. I journaled on the face and drew the features over the top of that. She has fabric-wrapped arms with cloth hands with a wire armature, that I again gessoed and painted. I did this so I could sculpt the hands easier—so they would hold the gold-painted baby in an offering gesture. Her feet are shoe charms, and her hair is needle-felted dyed wool roving.

She Gave Birth to a Sun

Linda Hansen

The artist writes:

> I spent a lot of time meditating on the meaning of goddess or what a goddess is. And I did what I usually do when I start researching; I reach for the handy dandy dictionary. Sometimes I "think" I know what a word means when there is actually more to it. When I looked up goddess, it said "a female deity or a woman of great beauty." What causes a woman to be beautiful? Love, fulfillment, and pregnancy were words that came to my mind. I liked her fullness; I felt she had a "ripe"-looking figure. With those ideas in mind, I started on Li's second goddess pattern.

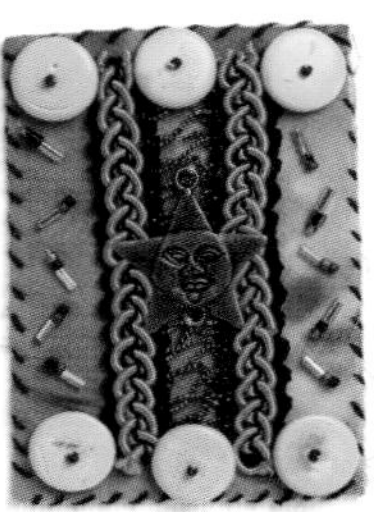

I wanted the colors to be juicy and vibrant. I have recently been enamored of what I think of as "India" colors: pinks, oranges, cool blues, and hot greens. I went though my stash of batik fabrics and found the perfect material containing all those colors. This enabled me to be unhindered in my choice of embellishments.

After I made the body, I glued a paper clay bezel that I had created from a mold of a stained glass piece. I beaded around it to secure it and give it a more continuous look. Beaded sunbeams were next. I went on to bead the doll across the body and down the legs; the star beads were a birthday present from my son.

I wanted her hands to convey joy and thankfulness, so I sculpted them out of paper clay, and added lots of layers of gesso and finally shimmering blue paint. Heart jewels are in her hands. Her arms were wrapped with lots of fantastic, fun fibers.

As is my practice with most of my dolls, the head was developed last. I wanted her facial expression to be serene and peaceful so that is why she is posed with her eyes shut. It is a trusting, relaxed pose. Her hair of dyed wool roving was needle-felted in. And last but not least, I added lots of beads to show off her swanlike neck, which is echoed by her long wired-up hair.

Garden Goddess

Barb and Doug Keeling

The artists write:

> "I am the Garden Goddess,
>
> I wear my flowers well.
>
> I didn't need to say that,
>
> For I'm sure that you can tell."
>
> We are a husband and wife team. Doug designed the head and hands. All the doll embellishment is designed and executed by Barb. The fiber is wool roving, soy silk wool, and knitting yarn. The fiber is twisted, bent, twirled, squeezed, pounded, knitted, and in general, lovingly and creatively formed into shapes and done as "emfeltishment." The goddess does indeed wear her garden well.

Damsel of Darkness

Elizabeth McGrath

The artist writes:

> Li's doll was a real challenge for me. Not that I think ill of people who like fairies, goddesses, princesses, angels, and things of that nature, but I myself can't stand anything of the sort. So the task of creating a goddess doll was a real stretch from what I normally like to do . . . how would I turn a goddess into a devil?
>
> Because I can't sew, Li was gracious enough to provide me with the doll body. I liked the fact that her legs were sewn together. It gave her a real turn-of-the-twentieth-century feel, not to mention virginal qualities! I also liked that there were wire arms, which are perfect for making tentacles. The first thing I did was paint her all black. I sculpted a head out of Magic Sculpt (a two-part epoxy putty) and embedded glass taxidermy eyes. I airbrushed her and dressed her with scraps that I had around the studio, which was the best part. It actually was quite easy turning a goddess into a devil; give it a try sometime!

namba teeke
LEG Cut 4
Leave open
Leave gap
HEAD Cut 2
Leave open
UNDERNOSE Cut 1
BODY Cut 4
Leave open
SNOOT Cut 2
Bridge
Leave open
Leave open
Leave gap for one seam only

namba teeke
Leave open
FOOT PAD Cut 4
EYE Cut 2
Leave gap
ARM Cut 4
EMBROIDERED MOUTH

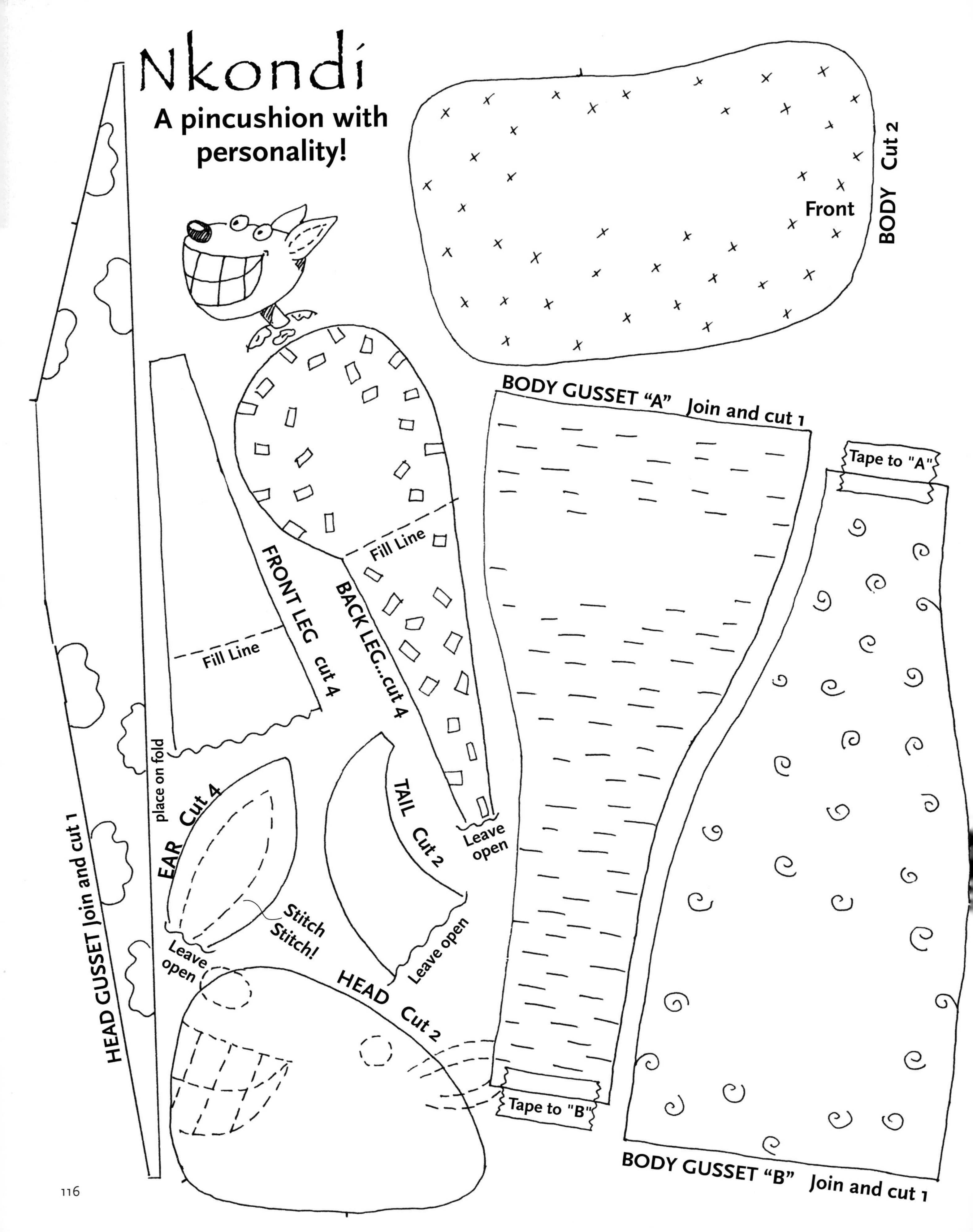
Nkondi
A pincushion with personality!
BODY Cut 2
Front
BODY GUSSET "A" Join and cut 1
Tape to "A"
FRONT LEG cut 4
Fill Line
BACK LEG...cut 4
Fill Line
place on fold
EAR Cut 4
Stitch Stitch!
Leave open
TAIL Cut 2
Leave open
Leave open
HEAD Cut 2
Tape to "B"
HEAD GUSSET Join and cut 1
BODY GUSSET "B" Join and cut 1

Doodle Blank

Photocopy at 200% for a 5½" × 8½" (14.0 × 21.6 cm) doodle blank

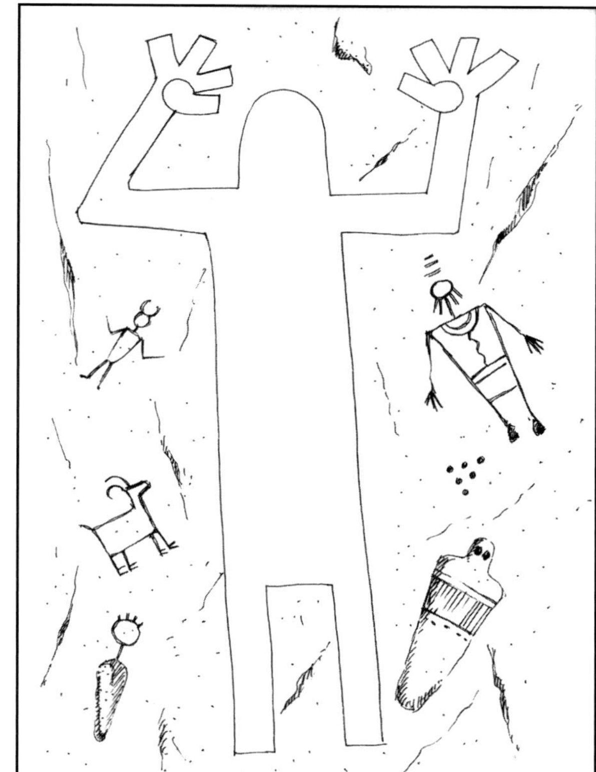

Wupatki

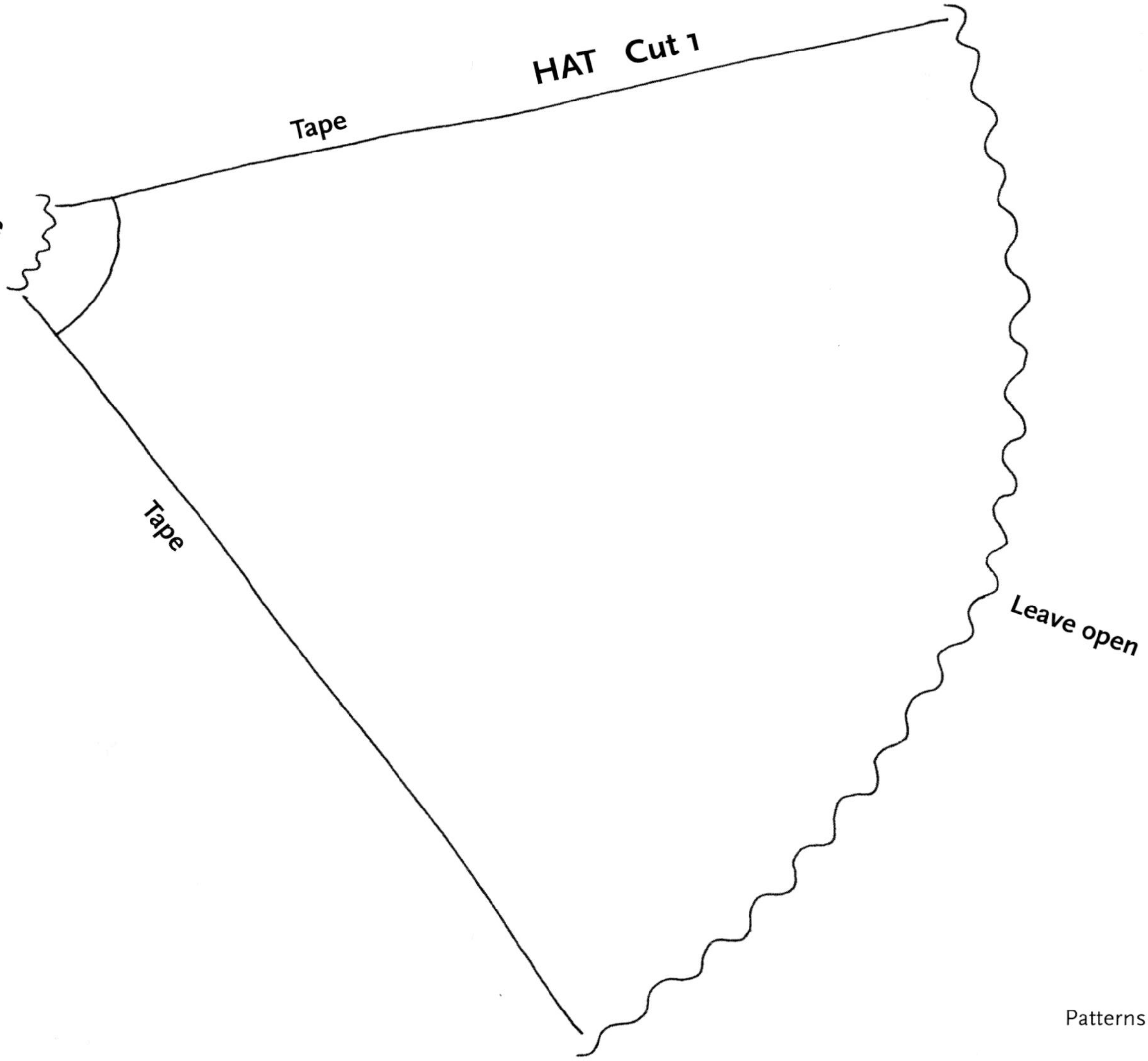

HAT Cut 1

Tape

Leave open

Tape

Leave open

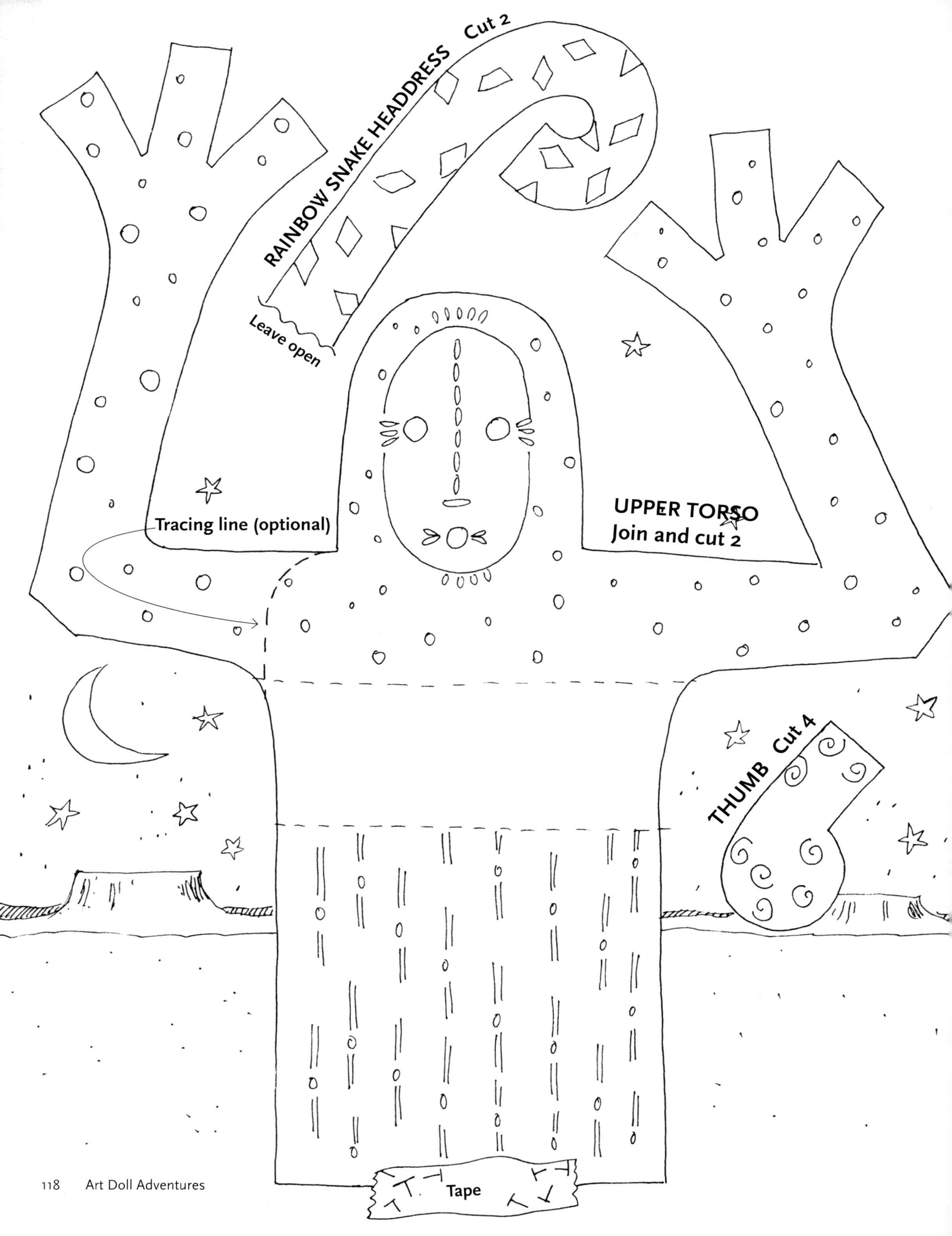
RAINBOW SNAKE HEADDRESS Cut 2
Leave open
Tracing line (optional)
UPPER TORSO
Join and cut 2
THUMB Cut 4
Tape

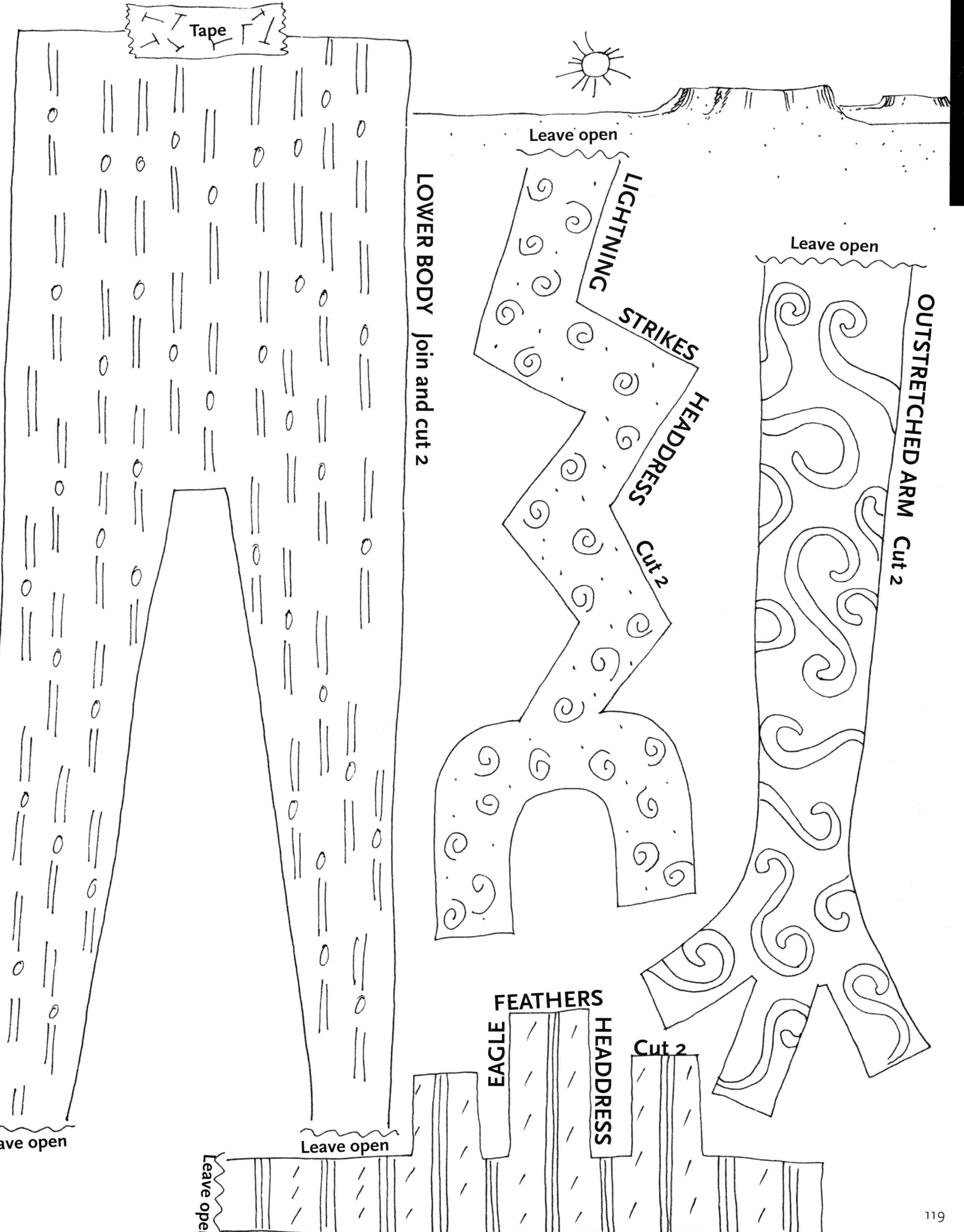
Tape
LOWER BODY Join and cut 2
Leave open
Leave open
Leave open
LIGHTNING STRIKES HEADDRESS
Cut 2
Leave open
OUTSTRETCHED ARM Cut 2
EAGLE FEATHERS HEADDRESS
Cut 2
Leave open
Leave open

Our Lady of Eureka

Leave open

Leave Open

Great goddess belly

Skinny minny belly

Leave gap

OUR LADY OF EUREKA BODY FRONT STRAIGHT LEG Cut 1

OUR LADY OF EUREKA BODY BACK STRAIGHT LEG Cut 1

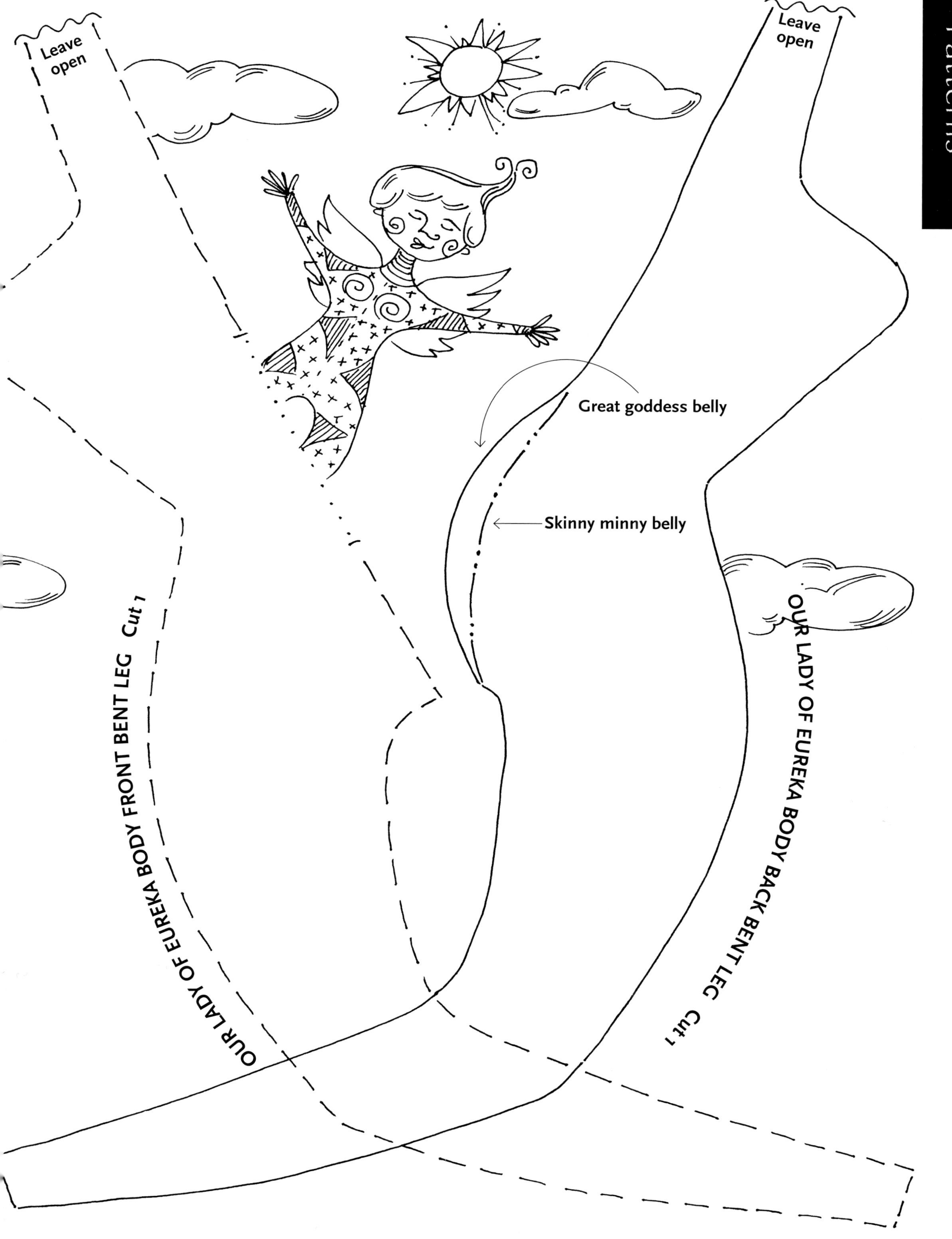
Leave open
Leave open
Great goddess belly
Skinny minny belly
OUR LADY OF EUREKA BODY FRONT BENT LEG Cut 1
OUR LADY OF EUREKA BODY BACK BENT LEG Cut 1

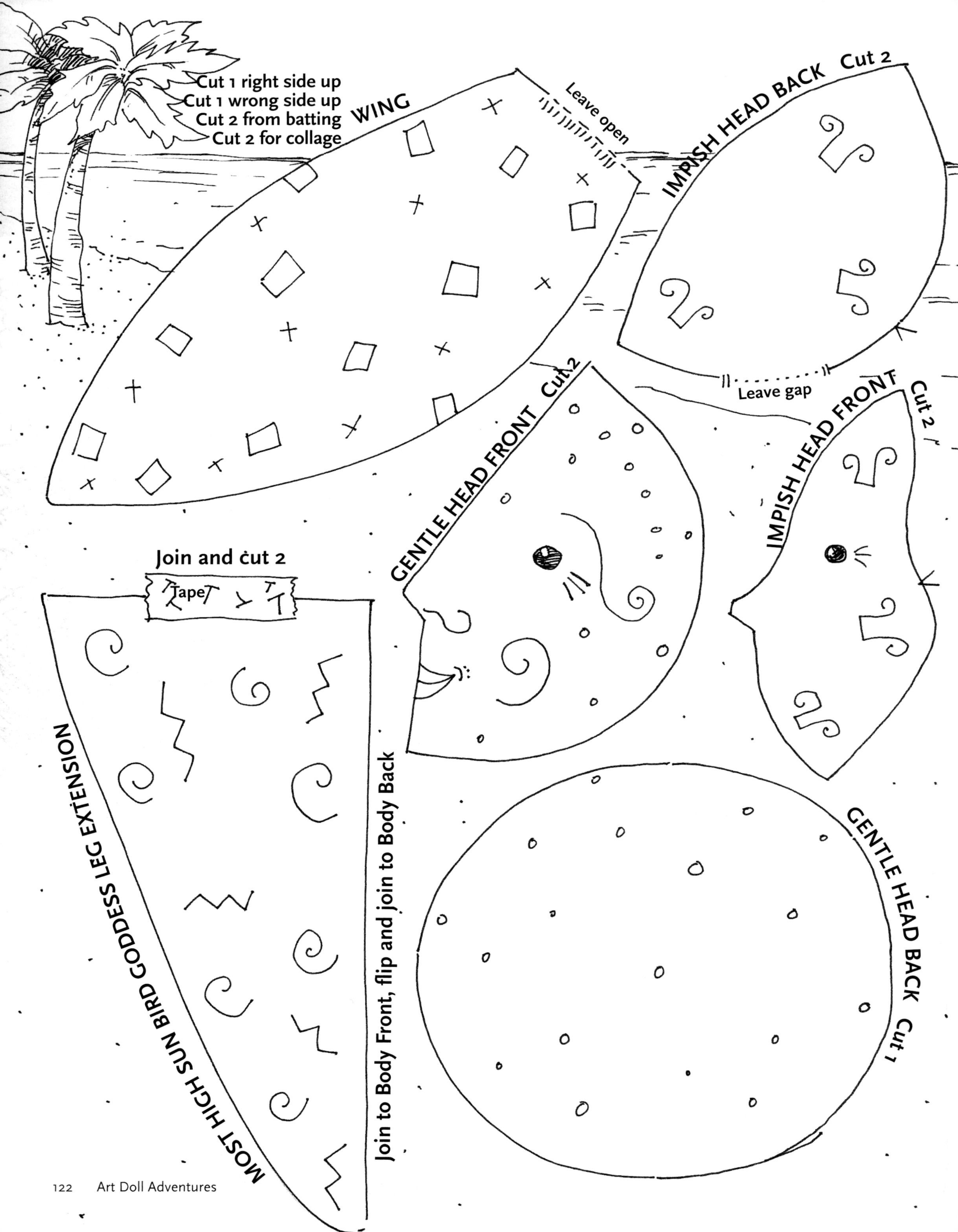
Cut 1 right side up
Cut 1 wrong side up
Cut 2 from batting
Cut 2 for collage
WING
Leave open
IMPISH HEAD BACK Cut 2
Leave gap
GENTLE HEAD FRONT Cut 2
IMPISH HEAD FRONT Cut 2
Join and cut 2
Tape
MOST HIGH SUN BIRD GODDESS LEG EXTENSION
Join to Body Front, flip and join to Body Back
GENTLE HEAD BACK Cut 1

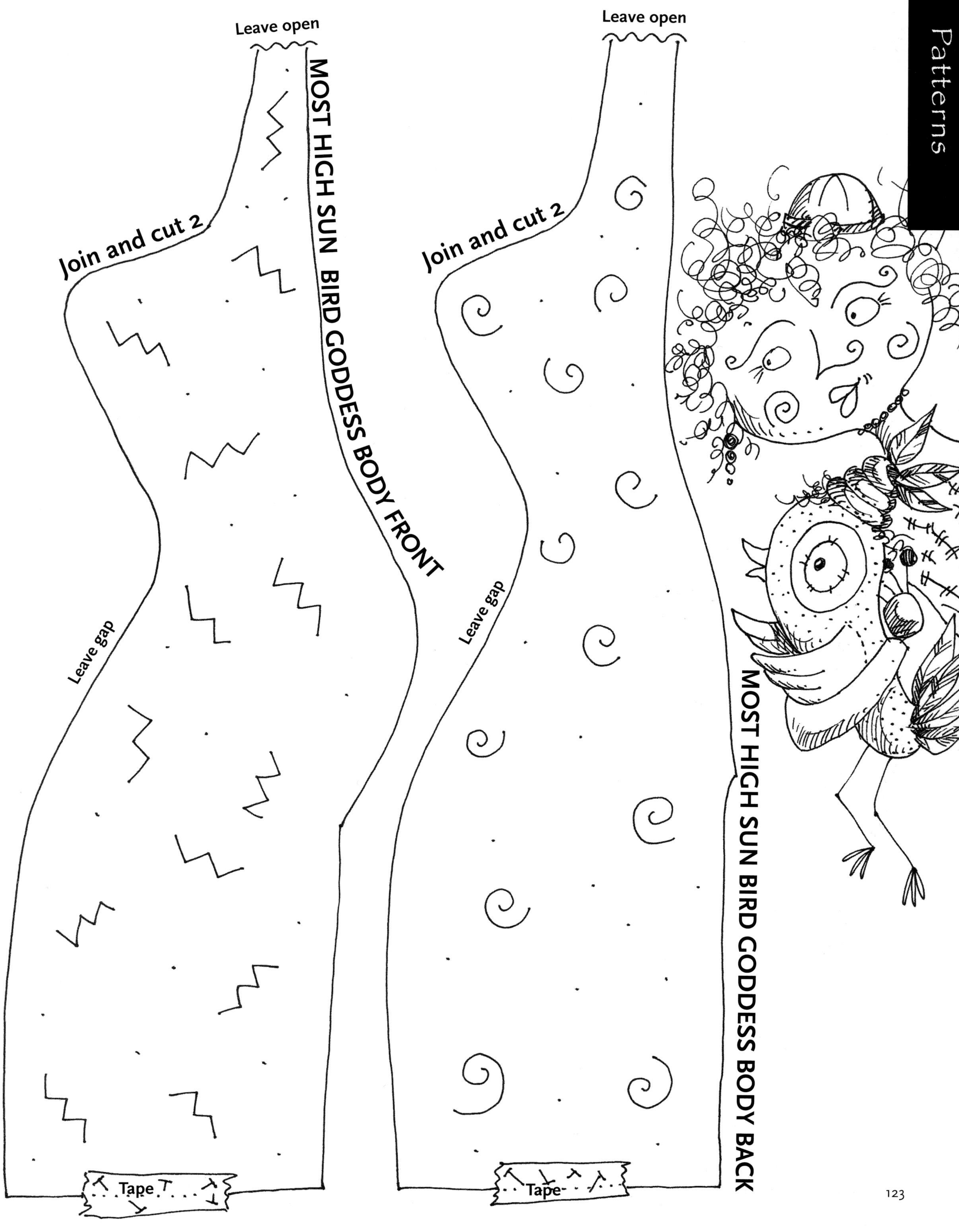
Leave open
Join and cut 2
MOST HIGH SUN BIRD GODDESS BODY FRONT
Leave gap
Tape
Leave open
Join and cut 2
Leave gap
MOST HIGH SUN BIRD GODDESS BODY BACK
Tape

Blue Chickie of Happiness

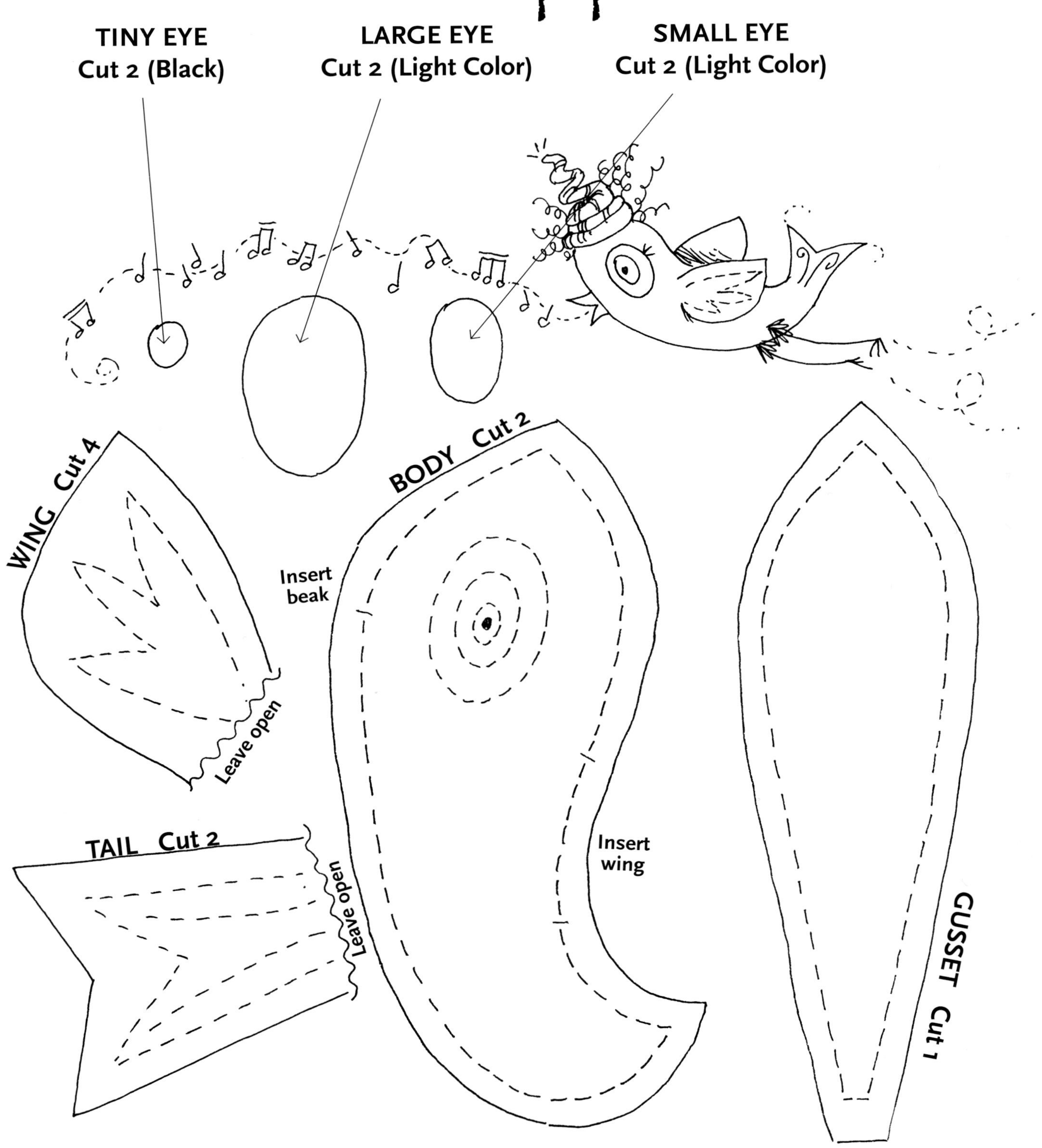

Resources

United States

CHEAP JOE'S ART STUFF
800.227.2788
www.cheapjoes.com
Art supplies

DOLLMAKER'S JOURNEY
7406 Shady Palm Dr.
Springfield, VA 22153 USA
703.569.7072
www.dollmakersjourney.com
Patterns, books, supplies for the contemporary doll artist

DOLLSTREET DREAMERS
www.dollstreetdreamers.com
Great classes, great community

EQUILTER.COM
www.equilter.com
Fabric

KEELING'S KRAFTS
www.keelingskrafts.com
Easy punch embroidery and cloth doll supplies and patterns

LI HERTZI DESIGN
300 Carlsbad Village Dr.
#108A-272
Carlsbad, CA 92008 USA
www.lihertzidesign.com
Patterns and classes

LION BRAND YARNS
www.lionbrand.com

MEINKE TOY
PMB #411, 55 E. Long Lake Rd.
Troy, MI 48085 USA
www.meinketoy.com

PMC DESIGNS
9019 Stargaze Ave.
San Diego, CA 92129 USA
858.484.5118
www.pmcdesigns.com
Patterns, tools, newsletters, classes, one-of-a-kind dolls

ROBERTSONS' ENTERPRISES
PO Box 357
Dolores, CO 81323 USA
970.882.3389
Hard-to-find cloth doll supplies catalog; Send $3.00 for the catalog.

RUPERT, GIBBON & SPIDER
PO Box 425
Healdsburg, CA 95448 USA
800.442.0455
www.jacquardproducts.com
Jacquard products: Dye-Na-Flow, Lumiere, and textile paints

Canada

BOBBINS 'N BEARS
#108 561 Johnson St.
Victoria, BC V8W 1M2 Canada
250.370.0633
www.bobbinsstudio.com
Fabrics, dyes and paints, beads, stabilizers, mohair, patterns

OPUS FRAMING & ARTS
800.663.6953
www.opusframing.com
Jacquard products, books, workshops

Australia

ANNE'S GLORY BOX
60 Beaumont St., Hamilton
NSW 2303 Australia
61.2.4961.6016
www.annesglorybox.com.au
Fabrics, dyes and paints, beads, books, stabilizers, mohair

THE THREAD STUDIO
6 Smith St., Perth
Western Australia 6000 Australia
61.8.9227.1561
www.thethreadstudio.com
Threads, stabilizers, paints, books, online classes

YADENO FIBRE CRAFT
35 Lake Dr., Meringandan
Queensland 4352 Australia
61.07.4696.9329
www.yadenofibrecraft.com.au

New Zealand

DESTINATION ART
31 Ramshaw Ln.
Arrowtown 9196 New Zealand
www.destinationart.co.nz
Jacquard products, Angelina, books, silk dyes

ZIG ZAG
8 Cherry Pl., Casebrook,
Christchurch New Zealand
www.2dye4.co.nz
Jacquard products, rubber stamps, Prismacolor pencils

United Kingdom

ART VAN GO
1 Stevenage Rd., Knebworth
Herts SG3 6AN England
44.01438.814946
www.artvango.co.uk
Jacquard products, Stewart Gill paints, books

CRAFTY NOTIONS
PO Box 6141
Newark NG24 2FQ England
44.01636.700862
www.craftynotions.com
Stabilizers, paints, Angelina fibers, beads and bead supplies, books

FIBRECRAFTS AND GEORGE WEIL
Old Portsmouth Rd.
Peasmarsh, Guildford
Surrey GU3 1LZ England
www.fibrecrafts.com
Paints, Angelina, books, workshops

THE PICTURE PLACE
(formerly The Yorkshire Art Store)
10 Market Pl.
Picering, North Yorkshire YO 187AA England
44.01751.475660
www.yorkshireartstore.co.uk
Jacquard products, paints, books

Europe

ZIJDELINGS
The Hague, The Netherlands
www.zijdelings.com
Jacquard products, books, fabrics, workshops

Further Reading

Fill your eyes and mind with books and magazines, listed by relevance to our chapters.

Chapter 2: Namba Teeke

ART DOLL QUARTERLY
www.stampington.com

PRIMITIVISM IN 20TH CENTURY ART
Edited by William Rubin
(Museum of Modern Art, 2002)
ISBN 0-87070-534-2

THE COLORS OF AFRICA
Duncan Clarke
(Thunder Bay Press, 2000)
ISBN 1-57145-264-8

Chapter 3: Kondi

1-2-3 EMBROIDERY: EASY PROJECTS FOR ELEGANT LIVING
Ellen Moore Johnson
(Quarry Books, 2003)
ISBN 1-56496-475-2

TRIBAL ARTS: AFRICA, OCEANIA, SOUTHEAST ASIA
Bérénice Geoffroy-Schneiter
(Vendome Press)
ISBN 0-86565-215-5

Chapter 4: Wupatki

CLOTH PAPER SCISSORS
A wonderful fiber arts and mixed-media magazine that any ATC artist will not be able to put down!
www.clothpaperscissors.com

LEGACY ON STONE: ROCK ART OF THE COLORADO PLATEAU AND FOUR CORNERS REGION
Sally J. Cole
(Johnson Books, 1990)
ISBN 1-55566-074-6

ROCK ART OF THE AMERICAN SOUTHWEST
Scott Thybony and Fred Hirschmann
(Graphic Arts Center Publishing Company, 1999)
ISBN 1-55868-467-0

SOUTHWEST ART
An art magazine that delves deep into all kinds of Southwest art.
www.southwestart.com

THOSE WHO CAME BEFORE: SOUTHWESTERN ARCHAEOLOGY IN THE NATIONAL PARK SYSTEM
Robert H. Lister and Florence C. Lister
(Southwest Parks & Monuments Association, 1993)
ISBN 1-87785-638-X

Chapter 5: Our Lady of Eureka!

QUILTING ARTS MAGAZINE
A beautiful and inspirational fiber magazine.
www.quiltingarts.com

THREADS MAGAZINE
Full of inspiration and new techniques for the fiberoholic!
www.threadsmagazine.com

CIVILIZATION OF THE GODDESS
Marija Alseikaite Gimbutas
(Harper San Francisco, 1991)
ISBN 0-06250-368-5

SANCTUARIES OF THE GODDESS: THE SACRED LANDSCAPES AND OBJECTS
Peg Streep
(Bulfinch Press, 1994)
ISBN 0-82121-976-6

COLLAGE FOR THE SOUL
Holly Harrison and Paula Grasdal
(Quarry Books, 2003)
ISBN 1-56496-962-2

CREATIVE CLOTH DOLL MAKING
Patti Medaris Culea
(Quarry Books, 2003)
ISBN 1-56496-942-8

Contributing Artists

INEZ BRASCH page 41
inezdb@mindspring.com
www.PictureTrail.com/InezBrasch
Inez Brasch has a degree in fine arts from The Ohio State University. Before having children, she worked as a commercial artist. She began creating dolls in 1990. Though she is comfortable with all media she prefers cloth and polymer or air drying clays.

PATTI MEDARIS CULEA pages 38-39
patti@pmcdesigns.com
www.PMCDesigns.com
Patti has been creating original cloth dolls for more than 20 years. When her two daughters were little, she went from fine arts to making cloth dolls. Her daughters grew up, but thankfully Patti continued thrilling the world with her cloth doll creations. She and her husband, John, live in San Diego.

She has authored four books with Rockport Publishers/Quarry Books, Creative Cloth Doll Making, Creative Cloth Doll Faces, Creative Cloth Doll Couture, and Creative Cloth Doll Beading. Her work has been included in a number of books and magazines.

SUE FARMER, page 37
sufarmer@iafrica.com
Sue arrived in Central Africa from England at the age of 6 and grew up on a small holding of 10 acres, the lone daughter with three brothers. Living 10 miles from the nearest town meant the family lived a somewhat solitary existence and, as a result, learned to amuse themselves. Her mother taught her to use a treadle machine and by age 11, she was sewing simple items. She has always found pleasure in working with fabric, so it was natural that dressmaking should become her main source of income.

She moved with her family (husband and two children) to South Africa in 1978, where she worked for the Nico Malan Opera House in Cape Town as a costumier for 5 years. She then opened her own costume shop, which she ran for 18 years.

Though dolls were not a part of her childhood at all, she can certainly remember longing for one. She was drawn to doll-making after being inspired by a book she bought in a London shop, and has been making dolls for her own pleasure ever since.

CODY GOODIN, page 40
codyart@fuse.net
www.codygoodin.com
Cody Goodin was raised in Kentucky. He is a sight-impaired artist (which means he is legally blind) and has a B.A. degree in fine art and theater design from Thomas More College. He has taken graduate level classes in fine art at the University of Cincinnati. He has been a sales associate at Lance's Art Supplies on Calhoun Street for the last 16 years. For the past 21 years he has been a working professional artist. He likes painting in acrylics and creating mixed-media pieces which incorporate fiber and clay. He teaches workshops and private classes. His work can be seen in a variety of collections throughout the world. Currently, he is represented by 7th Street Gallery in Newport, Kentucky, Crone Cottage Gift and Gallery in Bellevue, Kentucky, Urban Eden in Cincinnati, Ohio, and works in a studio at the Essex Studios in Cincinnati, Ohio.

LINDA HANSEN, pages 110-111
shansenwa@earthlink.net
www.picturetrail.com/missmabel
Linda has always been a "creator". Her first dolls were fuchsia blossoms that she thought looked liked diminutive dancers, at six years old. She is a self-taught, mixed-media artist who incorporates drawing, beading, painting, sculpting, stamping, sewing, paper making, fabric dyeing, and soon, she hopes, bookbinding.

She strives to give movement to all her dolls and is currently exploring marionette and puppet making. She lives with her quilt artist husband, three charming kids, eleven pampered chickens, and one beloved cat, on 3½ acres in a small town in Washington State.

JAN HAYMAN, page 109
jansdesigns@cox.net
Jan Hayman has been making dolls for about four years, with experience in wearable art. She was a designer for the Fairfield Fashion show and many of her garments won awards in major quilt shows. As she moved into doll making, creating garments on a smaller scale was right up her alley. She enjoys using techniques from beading, garment-making, and painting in her dolls.

JUDITH HARMON HERTZI, page 82
jjhertzi@webtv.net
Judi Hertzi is a painter who has exhibited nationally and her work is included in public and private collections. Throughout her long career as a teacher and artist, she became familiar with many styles of painting and has experimented extensively with batik techniques and the more traditional painter's mediums. She has created a unique, expressive style combining wax, colored ink, and acrylic.

She teaches adults and children in her studio with a variety of paint and print media. She also works in clay. In this extremely creative environment, students are encouraged to find their own way of expressing their thoughts and their environment. (Judi is Li's mother!)

BARB AND DOUG KEELING, page 112
www.keelingskrafts.com
Barb and Doug Keeling have been in the fiber art business for nearly 30 years (and married for 49). They have designed countless cloth doll patterns and done television craft demonstrations. They attend craft, sewing, quilt, doll, and fiber shows, demonstrating how to use various unique products. They also teach cloth doll making and have designed several cloth doll face books. Many of their dolls and art pieces have appeared in national magazines.

KATHY KENNY, page 81
Kkenney@neo.rr.com
Kathy Kenny is a life-long doll maker who enjoys experimenting with new, freer ways to play. She currently lives with her husband in Kent, Ohio, surrounded by wild gardens and a skittish group of stray cats. As a retired graphic artist, she spends her days playing with paper and fiber, working in her garden, and reading her way through an evergrowing stack of books. Slowly her art is taking on the same no-rules approach as her life. It's the best of times!

ELIZABETH MCGRATH, page 113
www.elizabethmcgrath.com
Influenced by a Roman Catholic upbringing, punk rock, Erte, and Edward Gorey, Hollywood native Elizabeth McGrath is one of her generation's more unique and prolific artists. She creates in a number of media and materials with undeniable artistry and imagination. Her paintings are haunted whispers of color that depict subtly dangerous creatures that creep toward the edge of the canvas. Her stitched and bandaged dolls and toys are a united army of soft strangeness, and her mixed-media dioramas are isolated freak shows displaying rotting, subhuman figures luxuriously dressed for your pleasure or contempt.

LESLIE MOLEN, page 108
www.rootie.com
Leslie has been a cloth doll artist for fifteen years. Her one-of-kind work is shown in galleries and museums around the world. Leslie is the owner of ROotie StudiO, which consists of a pattern line and dollmaking classes, which are available through her website. She teaches internationally. In 2006, Leslie was inducted into NIADA, a juried international group of doll artists. She is thrilled to be involved with a group of such highly talented people. She lives in Denver with her ever-supportive husband, Mark, and her kitty, Isabella Sunshine.

JOHN MURPHY, page 83
www.stupidcreatures.com
John Murphy lives in Asheville, North Carolina, where he runs the Stupid Creatures Toy Co., best known for its custom sock monster service, the Stupid Creatures (www.stupidcreatures.com). Murphy began his career in toy design in 2003 after a failed attempt to make a traditional sock monkey produced a disturbing, evil looking monster named Albertine. He has customers all over the world and throughout the U.S. who have commissioned custom Stupid Creatures. With new associate and monster design supergenius Ian Dennis (out of Winston-Salem, North Carolina), he fills custom and wholesale orders, teaches sock creature classes, and produces new work for shows. Murphy currently illustrates with writer Brandon Mise of Asheville, North Carolina, a graphic novel called Being: The Adventures of One Uther Smith. *Their comic book label, Bimini Comics (www.biminicomics.com) currently has two titles in production. He is the author of a how-to book,* Stupid Sock Creatures *(Lark Books, 2005).*

ROSIE ROJAS, pages 60, 84
www.asinglerosedolls.com
Rosie lives and works in San Antonio, Texas. She has been making dolls for more than 20 years and works with polymer clays, stone clay, fabric, and mixed media.

Through her blend of computerized images, freeform embellishing, and her use of color and texture, Rosie turns her dolls into canvasses of creativity and self expression. Rosie also teaches doll making in workshops and online. Rosie's dolls have been featured in several publications, exhibits, and local and international shows. Her work can be found for sale in several local galleries and on her website, and she teaches several workshops around the country each year.

RIVKAH ROSENFELD, page 85
Rivkahrosenfeld@gmail.com
www.rivkahrosenfeld.googlepages.com
www.dollmakersmuse.blogspot.com
Rivkah is a mixed-media doll artist who resides in Rehovot, Israel. She and her family made their way to the Middle East from Seattle, Washington, in 2002. Fascinated (and sometimes frustrated) by her exotic surroundings and culture, she has learned how to internalize it all by incorporating it into her art.

Rivkah's dolls have been exhibited around Israel and in the U.S., and appear in Art Doll Quarterly *magazine, Patti Medaris Culea's book,* Creative Cloth Doll Faces *(Quarry Books, 2005), and online doll art publications. Rivkah's greatest source of encouragement is her husband, Ariel, who greatly appreciates and encourages her and her artistry.*

ISABELLA ZAMBEZI, page 61
createorama@gmail.com
Isabella is an illustrator, artist, and doll maker.

About the Author

Lisa Li Hertzi is a professional artist and illustrator living in southern California. She designs an eclectic line of cloth doll patterns, teaches online workshops, obsessively blogs, designs cycling clothing, and runs the art department for Squadra Inc. USA. Her work has appeared in galleries, books, private collections, and on the backs of countless cyclists all over the world.

Acknowledgments and Thank-Yous

Thanks to my wonderful family (Judi, Joe, Emily, Jeff, Ben, Grace, and Dan!) for putting up with hours of book talk and still ending the conversations with "I love you" and, of course, for all your support and love throughout the process.

Many thanks to Mary Ann Hall, editor supreme, patient teacher, taskmaster, and overall delightful person without whom this book would still be in my head. Thanks to the staff at Quarry Books and Susan Huxley for their skillful organizing of my wild ideas, to Bob Hirsch for his great photography, wily sense of humor and happy demeanor, and to the talented Patti Culea for putting me into her book and opening wide this new door! Thanks must also go to epb, who first suggested that I should try making a pattern, and to Carol Larson (Molly) for insisting that I teach on dollstreet then enthusiastically turning my ramblings and doodles into digital education.

Thanks to all of the artists in this book and to everyone who has ever made my dolls! You are brave and creative, and I love calling you kin!

Thanks to my wonderful, grounding friends Marty and Anna as well as my Sunday morning yoga buds and the teachers at the Yoga Center for keeping me sane and relatively fit during this amazing process.

And finally, thanks to Mr. Donellon, who said in the midst of a childhood grammar crisis, "You will write a book someday and this will all be worth it" and somehow, it stuck with me…